CB121064

BESS BRADFIELD
CAROL LETHABY

Series editors:
BEN GOLDSTEIN & CERI JONES

The BIG Picture

PRE-INTERMEDIATE A

Student's Book

Richmond

Richmond

Richmond Publishing ®
58 St Aldates
Oxford
OX1 1ST
United Kingdom

First Edition: 2011 / Reprinted: 2013
Split Edition: 2014

Publisher: Deborah Tricker
Content Development: Laura Miranda, Mary Todd, Kate Chomacki, Eleanor Clements
Managing Editor: Mary Todd
Editor: Kate Chomacki, Rhona Snelling, Jo Kent
Proofreader: Hazel Geatches
'Skills Development' Sections: Bess Bradfield
Progress Tests: Bess Bradfield
Audio Production: Motivation Sound Studios
Cover Design: Pentacor Book Design, Lorna Heaslip
Design & Layout: Lorna Heaslip, Rob Briggs, Dave Kuzmicki
Photo Researcher: Magdalena Mayo
Art Coordinators: Lorna Heaslip, Dave Kuzmicki
Illustrators: Richard Allen c/o Eye Candy Illustration Ltd., Francis Blake c/o Three-in-a-Box Ltd., Chris Davidson, Phil Hackett c/o Eye Candy Illustration Ltd., Matt Latchford c/o Advocate Art Ltd., Myles Talbot, Ron Wilson

Photos – Student's Book:
J. Jaime; J. V. Resino; S. Enríquez; S. Padura; M. Mayo; beargrylls.com; COMSTOCK; Corbis Images; DIGITAL BANK; Doug Savage/Savagechickens.com; EFE; The Bees/ Flickr.com; Aine D/Flickr.com; Alex E. Proimos/Flickr.com; Ampersandsyslexia/ Flickr.com; Jonrawlison/Flickr.com; Seb Ruiz/Flickr.com; GETTY IMAGES SALES SPAIN/Photos.com Plus; HIGHRES PRESS STOCK/AbleStock.com; I. Preysler; IBIZA FOTOESTUDIO/R. Martínez; ISTOCKPHOTO; Princeton.edu/-INA; JOHN FOXX IMAGES; Mark Boyle/justfortheloveofit.org; Lego ®; matthewsanford.com; NASA; SEIS X SEIS; Seth Shostak/SETI Institute; PA Photos; Mark Henley/Panos Pictures; Phiggles the Flying Scientist; c. 20thC. Fox/Everett/Rex Features; Rex Features/ Stephen Meddle; NBCUPHOTOBANK/Rex Features; Sun Media; Social Stock; Tamer Nakisci/Studionakisci.com; Alamy; Cortesía de Apple; M. Ortega/J. Frías; MATTON-BILD; Samsung; SERIDEC PHOTOIMAGENES CD/DigitalVision; ARCHIVO SANTILLANA; Wageningen UR

Photos – Workbook:
D. Sánchez; M. Mayo; F. Ontañón; F. Orte; I. Rovira; J. Escandell.com; J. Jaime; J. M.ª Barres; J. M.ª Escudero; Krauel; L. M. Iglesias; S. Enríquez; A. G. E. FOTOSTOCK; ALAMY; BLIZZARD ENTERTAINMENT; BRIDGEMAN ART LIBRARY; COVER/CORBIS; EFE/Tom Specht; EN.WIKIPEDIA/Markus Poessel; GETTY IMAGES SALES SPAIN/Photos.com Plus; HAMILTONS GALLERY/Alison Jackson; HIGHRES PRESS STOCK/AbleStock.com; I. Preysler; ISTOCKPHOTO; LOBO PRODUCCIONES /C. Sanz; Cortesía de Apple; MICHAEL HUGHES PHOTOGRAPHY; REX FEATURES; THREADLESS/Sean Dorgan; ARCHIVO SANTILLANA

Cover Photo:
Rice Paddy Fields in Southern China, aerial view
Getty Images Sales Spain/Jialiang Gao

We would like to thank the following reviewers for their valuable feedback which has made *The Big Picture* possible. We extend our thanks to the many teachers and students not mentioned here.

(Argentina): Cecilia Chiacchio, Ingrid Suhring; (Brazil): Ana Falcao, Virginia Garcia, Patricia McKay, Cynthia Phillipps, Bia Sousa; (Colombia): Kathleen Canal; (Italy): Morgan Cox, Karen Geiger, Sarah Stats; (Mexico): Emma Dominguez, Melissa Ferrin, Lupita Neve, Coral Ibarra Yunez; (Poland): Malgosia Adams, Marta Rosinska; (Spain): Vicki Anderson, Juan Carlos Araujo, Karen Dyer, Gabby Maguire, Fiona McClelland, Karin Rickatson, Almudena Verdugo Valcarce, Andy Walsh; (UK): Cathy Ellis, Howard Smith, Jonathan Stoddart

Dados Internacionais de Catalogação na Publicação (CIP)
(Câmara Brasileira do Livro, SP, Brasil)

Bradfield, Bess
The big picture, pre-intermediate : student's book/ workbook / Bess Bradfield, Carol Lethaby. -- São Paulo : Moderna, 2014. -- (The big picture)

1. Inglês - Estudo e ensino I. Lethaby, Carol. II. Título. III. Série.

13-13474 CDD-420.7

Índices para catálogo sistemático:
1. Inglês : Estudo e ensino 420.7

978-85-16-09145-3

RICHMOND PUBLISHING
EDITORA MODERNA LTDA.
Rua Padre Adelino, 758 — Belenzinho
São Paulo — SP — Brasil — CEP 03303-904
Central de atendimento ao usuário: 0800 771 8181
www.richmond.com.br
2013
Printed in Brazil

CONTENTS

1 SPEAKING THE SAME LANGUAGE

a

b

c

d

1 a Work in pairs. Look at the welcome signs. How many different languages can you see? Do you know what they are?

b Match signs a–f to the places where they could appear.

on a beach · on the side of a building · on a motorway · at a port · at a shopping centre · at a zoo

2 Work in pairs. How many languages can you say 'hello' and 'goodbye' in? Which country/countries do you associate with each language? Complete A in the KEY VOCABULARY PANEL.

3 a 1.1 Listen to Ellen and Ernesto talking about the languages they speak. Note the languages they mention.

Ellen: *Welsh* ....

Ernesto: *Guaraní* ....

b What similarities did you notice about the two speakers?

e

f

4 **a** Listen again and match the statements to Ellen, Ernesto or both.

1 There are two **official language**s. ....
2 I have two **first language**s. ....
3 Guaraní is my **mother tongue**. ....
4 A lot of people are **bilingual** in my country. ....
5 I learnt Spanish as a **second language**. ....
6 I learnt French as a **foreign language**. ....

b Match the words in **bold** with definitions 1–5 in B in the KEY VOCABULARY PANEL.

5 **a** Work in groups. Discuss the questions.

- What is your first language? Do you have a second language? Do you speak any other languages?
- What are the official languages in your country? Are any other languages popular? Are people bilingual?
- Which languages would you like to learn? Why?
- Which language would you not like to learn? Why?

b Share your answers with the class.

KEY VOCABULARY

Languages

A Languages & countries

- Match the language to the country/countries. One country has two languages.

Arabic	Australia
Cantonese	Belgium
Dutch	Brazil
English	China
French	Egypt
Hindi	Holland
Japanese	India
Mandarin	Japan
Portuguese	Kenya
Spanish	Peru
Swahili	

- Can you think of more countries and languages?

B Words to describe languages

1 to speak two languages fluently and comfortably *to be* ....
2 the language the government uses on forms, on road signs and in school books
....
3 the language you spoke as a child OR the language you speak at home
.... OR ....
4 the language of government and business in the country where you live, which is not the same as your language
....
5 a language which is spoken in a different country
....

- PRACTISE THE PRESENT SIMPLE & PRESENT CONTINUOUS
- TALK ABOUT SPEAKING & LEARNING LANGUAGES

a

b

c

READING

1 Work in pairs. Look at the photos. Discuss the questions.

- Which countries do you think the photos show?
- Which languages do the people speak there?
- Can you think of three countries which have more than one official language?

2 a Read the article *Being bilingual*. Match the people to the photos.

b Read the article again. Complete the sentences with the correct name: Marcela, Robert, Wotoro or Brad.

1 *Robert* lives in a country where French is an important language.
2 .... is working as a teacher at the moment.
3 .... goes to school five days a week.
4 .... lives and works in two different countries.
5 .... uses French when he/she is teaching.
6 .... is learning a new language.
7 .... regularly travels to a different part of the same country.

Being bilingual

What's it like to be fluent in two or more languages? We interviewed four bilingual people to find out.

Marcela: 'I live in Tijuana in Mexico, but I work in San Diego in the USA five days a week. I speak English and Spanish well and I'm taking weekly Japanese classes at the moment. Sometimes I don't know how to say what I want to say in English, so I say it in Spanish. Luckily, most people I know speak both languages.'

Robert: 'I live in Belgium and I speak Flemish (which is like Dutch) and French. I live in Flanders and almost everyone here speaks Dutch and French. A lot of people also speak English, like me – I'm speaking English now! I visit the French-speaking part of Belgium every month because my grandmother lives there. A lot of people there don't know Flemish or English.'

Wotoro: 'There are over 60 languages in Kenya and there are two official languages, so it's common for people to speak at least three different languages – their mother tongue and English and Swahili. I speak Gikuyu with my family, English on Monday to Friday mornings when I go to school, and Swahili or Gikuyu when I buy things at the market. I think in all three languages. Right now, I'm thinking in English because I'm speaking English.'

Brad: 'I'm American, but I work at a French immersion school. I'm teaching beginner's French at the moment. I started to learn French when I was four and a half and then I majored in French at college and lived in France for a few years. Some people think that being bilingual makes you smarter. I don't know if that's true, but it's fun to know two languages.'

3 Work in groups. Discuss the questions.

- Are you bilingual?
- What would you enjoy/not enjoy about being bilingual?
- Do you know someone who is bilingual? Describe how he/she uses the two languages.

GRAMMAR

1 Look at the sentences in READING 2b again. Underline the verbs. Which are a) in the present simple? b) in the present continuous?

2 a Look at the GRAMMAR PANEL. Complete 1–3 with a–c.

a general truths or situations
b regular habits/routines
c things that are happening right now

b Find one more example of each of the uses 1–3 in the sentences in READING 2b. Write the examples in the GRAMMAR PANEL.

3 Complete the email with the correct form of the verbs. Explain your choice.

> Hi Misha,
>
> How are you? I'm really busy this term, I (1)*study / 'm studying* Arabic. It's really interesting, but it means I'm quite busy! I (2)*go / 'm going* to class every day for three hours. We (3)*work / 're working* on the alphabet at the moment. I love the Arabic script, it's so beautiful, but it's really difficult too! I (4)*spend / am spending* three hours every night practising my handwriting. It's like being at primary school again!
>
> (5)*Do you do / Are you doing* that online course at the moment? We really must meet up soon for a chat. Me and Toni usually (6)*meet / are meeting* for coffee every morning at about 10 o'clock. Do you want to join us? Tomorrow maybe?
>
> Text me! Corinne

4 a Write true sentences about you.

1 live / with my family
2 study / a foreign language / at the moment
3 take / a summer holiday / every year
4 like / Italian food
5 work / at the moment

b Find one person in the class who wrote the same as you for each of 1–5.

PRESENT SIMPLE & PRESENT CONTINUOUS

We usually use the **present simple** to talk about:

(1) *general truths or situations*
I live in Tijuana.
....

(2) ....
I go to class on Saturdays.
....

We use the **present continuous** to talk about:

(3) ....
Right now, I'm studying English.
....

We often use these time expressions with the present simple: *usually, often, every day, every night*

We often use these time expressions with the present continuous: *at the moment, (right) now, these days*

See page 140 for grammar reference and more practice.

NOTICE *RIGHT NOW*

Use *right now* to talk about things happening at the time of speaking. *I'm reading this right now.*

PRONUNCIATION: final *-s*

1 1.2 Listen to four people talking about learning a language. Which skill does each speaker think is most important?

listening reading speaking writing

2 a 1.3 Listen to the verbs. How do we pronounce -s? Match 1–3 to a–c.

1 /s/	2 /z/	3 /ɪz/
a writes speaks	b practises uses watches notices	c reads listens

b Add the verbs to 1–3.

changes helps loves makes needs plays puts teaches thinks wants

3 1.4 Listen and check.

1.2 GOOD TALKING TO YOU

- PRACTISE QUESTIONS
- DISCUSS FREE-TIME ACTIVITIES

a

b

c

d

SPEAKING

1 a Match photos a–d to situations 1–4.

1 interviewing someone for a job
2 going on a first date
3 talking to a good friend
4 meeting someone for the first time

b What do people usually talk about in situations 1–4? Think of three ideas for each situation.

2 a 1.5 Listen and match conversations e–h to the situations.

b Listen again. Tick the things people talk about in conversations e–h.

	e	f	g	h
Name				
Age				
Nationality				
Languages you speak				
Hobbies				
Recent events				
Skills and experience				
Personality				
People you both know				
Family				

GRAMMAR

1 a Read the questions from the conversations in SPEAKING 2. Can you remember the answers?

1 When do you play squash?
2 Who do you play with?
3 Why do you want to work here?
4 How many languages do you speak?
5 Are you a student?
6 What kind of music do you like?
7 Do you like going to concerts?
8 How often do you go?

b 1.5 Listen again and check.

2 Which two questions in 1 have the answer 'yes' or 'no'?

3 a Underline six question words and expressions (e.g. *When*) in 1a.

b Complete 1–6 in the GRAMMAR PANEL.

4 a Circle the main verbs and the auxiliary verbs (*Do/Does*) in 1a.

b Choose the correct option for 7 and 8 in the GRAMMAR PANEL.

Intonation in questions

1.6 Listen to four questions. Does the person's voice go up ⤴ or down ⤵ at the end of

1 yes/no questions?
2 questions with a question word?

Listen again and repeat.

5 Write questions for the answers.

My favourite actor is Johnny Depp.
Who is your favourite actor?

1 I like horror films and comedies.
2 My favourite singer is Shakira.
3 My birthday is on 11 May.
4 I live on Calle de la Cruz in Vigo, Spain.
5 I watch TV every night.
6 I want to learn English because it is useful for my job.
7 I speak two languages, English and Spanish.

6 Write four more questions you would like to ask the person sitting next to you.

7 a Work in pairs. Ask and answer your questions.

b What did you learn about your partner?

QUESTIONS

Types of questions

- ***Yes/No* questions**
  We answer the questions with 'yes' or 'no'.
  Are you a student? (Yes, I am./No, I'm not.)
  Do you work here? (Yes, I do. /No, I don't.)
- **Question words/expressions (*Wh-* questions)**
  We form other questions with question words or expressions.

Where....... *(places)*,
(1) W.................. *(people)*
(2) W.................. *(kind of) (things)*
(3) W.................. *(time)*
(4) W.................. *(reason)*
(5) H.................. o.................. *(frequency)*
(6) H.................. m.................. *(number)*

***Who** is your teacher?* ***Where** do you live?*

Word order in questions

In present simple questions, we put *do* or *does* (7) *after / before* the subject, and the main verb (8) *after / before* the subject.

***Do** you like your job?* *Where **does** he live?*

We don't use *do* or *does* in questions with *be*.

***Are** you English?* *Who **is** that man?*

See page 140 for grammar reference and more practice.

VOCABULARY: free time

1 Work in pairs. Look at the photos. Discuss the questions.

- Which of the things do you enjoy doing?
- Is there anything you don't enjoy doing? Why?

a

d

b

e

c

f

2 a Complete the activities. Use a dictionary to help you.

1 l*i*stening to *musi*c
2 going t... the gy...
3 s...rfing the int.......net
4 pl...ying f.......tb...ll
5 having friends r.......nd
6 eating ...ut at rest.......r.......ts
7 going clu.......ing
8 r.......ding the n.......sp.......er
9 sho.......ing in town

b Match six activities to the photos.

3 Read the questions and make notes for your answers.

- What do you usually do in your free time in the evenings?
- What do you usually do in your free time at the weekend?

4 a Ask the questions in 3 to students in your class. Make notes of their answers.

b Who is the most similar to you? What are the most popular free-time activities?

1.3 Is there anybody out there?

Reading & Speaking

1 **a** Look at the photo. Where is it and what can you see there?

b Quickly read the online article about SETI and check your answer.

2 Read the article again. Match the Frequently Asked Questions (FAQS) about SETI to the answers.

3 Read the article again and answer the questions.

1 What is SETI looking for?
2 Are SETI methods the same now as in 1960?
3 What is the Allen Telescope Array?
4 Where are there SETI projects?
5 What is the difference between SETI and METI?
6 How long will the message from Ukraine to Gliese 581 take to arrive?

SETI INSTITUTE

Search GO

Home | About us | SETI | Astrobiology | Education | Publications | Calendar | Support us | TeamSETI | Contact us

FAQS about The Search for Extra-Terrestrial Intelligence (SETI) organisation

1 Do we send messages to other planets?
2 What is SETI?
3 How many people are part of SETI?
4 When did SETI begin?
5 Why don't we try harder to communicate with aliens?
6 What does SETI do?

a Are we alone? This is the question human beings asked when we first realised that there are other planets in our solar system. SETI is the name of the organisation that looks for evidence of life in the universe. SETI projects use scientific methods to search for signals from beings on other planets.

b SETI began in 1960. The SETI methods and equipment are improving all the time. SETI researchers say that as the methods get better the chances of finding extra-terrestrial life also get better.

c SETI uses radio telescopes to try to find signals from other planets. The biggest project is the Allen Telescope Array which has 42 radio telescopes near San Francisco, California.

d Today there are 15,000 members of SETI in 60 countries on all seven continents of the world and there are SETI projects in the USA, Australia and Italy.

e SETI doesn't send signals into space; it only listens to find out if there are other life forms. The organisation that sends messages into space is METI ('Messaging to Extra-Terrestrial Intelligence').

f Many scientists don't think it is a good idea to send messages to other planets, because they think it is dangerous to tell other planets about the location of Earth. Sending messages to other planets is also very slow! The National Space Agency in Ukraine sent a message to the planet Gliese 581 in October 2008 and they won't receive this message until 2029.

4 Work in groups. Discuss the questions.

- Do you think SETI or METI is a good idea? Why/Why not?
- Do you think there is life on other planets? Why/Why not?
- Do you know about any theories or research into life on other planets?
- Would you like to talk to beings from other planets? What would you ask them?

VOCABULARY: communication

1 Complete the sentences with the correct form of the verbs in the box.

receive listen send tell

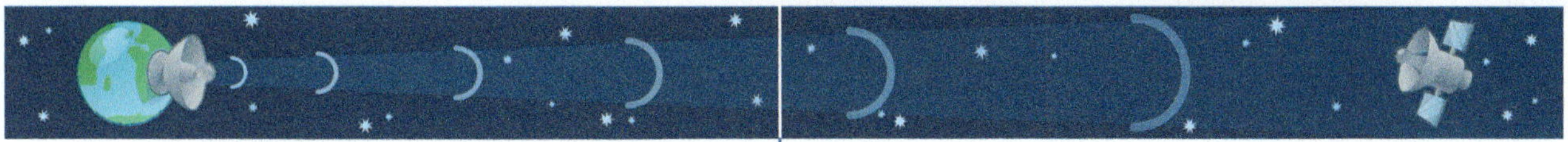

1 The organisation that .... messages into space is called METI.

2 Some scientists think it is dangerous to .... other planets about Earth.

3 SETI .... to find out if there are other life forms.

4 The planet Gliese 581 won't .... the message until 2029.

2 **a** Work in pairs. What is the difference between the expressions?

1 I usually tell *the truth* / *lies*.
2 I like talking *about* / *to* other people.
3 I like to write *about* / *to* my friends.
4 I like *listening to* / *hearing about* interesting news stories.

b Which option in each sentence describes you?

LISTENING & SPEAKING

1 Read about the *Earth Speaks* project. Answer the questions.

1 What is the purpose of the project?
2 What can people send?

2 1.7 Listen to this *Earth Speaks* message. Are the statements true or false? Correct the false statements.

1 They like living on Earth.
2 People are very selfish.
3 People on Earth like to know about other places.
4 They don't expect to hear from the other planet.

3 **a** Work in pairs. What do you want to tell aliens about Earth? Make your own message for the *Earth Speaks* project and record it or write it.

b Listen to or read all the messages. Which messages were the most serious/funniest and why?

Welcome to **Earth Speaks**, a research project that investigates this question:

'If we discover intelligent life beyond Earth, should we reply, and if so, what should we say?'

We invite people from around the world to send pictures, sounds and text messages that they want to send to other worlds. The project aims to answer two questions: Can we talk to aliens? What can we tell them?

a

b

c

TUNE IN

1 Work in pairs. Look at photos a–d. Where are the people and what are they doing?

2 1.8 Listen and match conversations 1–4 to the photos.

3 What is the problem in each conversation?

- speaking too quietly
- the person doesn't understand a word
- the person doesn't know how to say the word in English
- speaking too quickly

4 Listen again and complete the sentences.

1 Could you .... more ...., please?
2 I'm .... I didn't .... you.
3 What .... 'deposit slip' .... ?
4 How .... you .... it in .... ?

FOCUS ON LANGUAGE

5 Match the responses in 4 with a similar way of saying the same thing.

1 Can you repeat that, please?
2 Can you say it again, please?
3 What did you say?
4 I don't know what ... means.
5 What do you call this in English?

6 Match the two parts of these five conversations. Work in pairs. Practise saying them.

1 What do you call the things you use to read with?
2 What does 'Dutch' mean?
3 What did you say?
4 Sorry, I didn't hear you.
5 Could you say that again, please?

a Sorry. Is this better? Where are you from?
b I said – Do you want whipped cream with your coffee?
c Oh, do you mean 'glasses'?
d Sure. I asked if you would like a sandwich.
e It's the language of the Netherlands.

d

OVER TO YOU

7 Work in groups. Choose a new word. Get your group to describe it without saying the word.

What do you call it when someone is saying things that are not true?

8 Work in pairs. Student A, imagine you are staying with an English-speaking friend. You need one of the items in photos e–h. Explain what you need to student B, without saying the name of the item.

Student B, you have a friend staying with you. He/She needs one of the items in photos e–h. Listen and try to identify the item. Check your answer on page 158.

e

f

g

h

TUNE IN

1 Look at the advertisement. Do you think it's possible? How?

2 Work in groups. Discuss your own language-learning experiences.

- What languages have you tried to learn and why?
- When did you start? How successful were you?
- Which things made it easier/harder for you?

Learn a language in just six weeks with our new system. You'll be speaking French, German, Spanish or Japanese in just six weeks or your money back! No boring classes, no hours of grammar study – just learn to speak.

PREPARE FOR TASK

3 **a** Read the questionnaire extract. Which things are true for you? Which are not?

b Work in pairs. Compare your answers with your partner.

1 I'm learning English:
to get a better job / more money
to pass an exam
because I'm interested in language
to understand films and music
because my parents want me to
other reasons ___________

2 I'm interested in
speaking listening reading writing

3 I plan to study 2–4, 5–10, 11–15 hours a week outside class.

4 Read the list of study skills and say how each one can help you. Which ones do you do?

- study outside class
- watch films in English
- listen to music in English
- check your notes before/after class
- do your homework
- memorise vocabulary
- organise your lesson notes
- read books and magazines in English
- use a dictionary
- speak to English-speaking people

5 1.9 Listen to Sandra and Max talking about learning English this year. Complete the form.

	SANDRA	MAX
I plan to spend ... hours a week outside class practising English.		
I plan to...		
• watch films and TV		
• listen to music		
• read my notes before/after class		
• do homework		
• write down and study new vocabulary		
• read books and magazines		
• use a dictionary		
• practise exercises online		

6 Work in groups. Compare your answers and decide who you think has the best plan.

TASK

7 Complete the form with your own answers.

Name: ______

I plan to spend ... hours a week outside class practising English.	
I plan to...	
• watch films and TV	
• listen to music	
• read my notes before/after class	
• do homework	
• write down and study new vocabulary	
• read books and magazines	
• use a dictionary	
• practise exercises online	

8 Work in pairs. Talk about what you have written with your partner.

REPORT BACK

9 Work in groups or as a class. Compare language-learning plans. Who has the best plan?

➜ Go to Review A, Unit 1, p. 34 ➜ Go to Writing bank 1, p. 152

2 BACK TO NATURE

a

c

b

d

1 Work in groups. Look at the photos. What are the people doing?

2 Use the phrases in A in the KEY VOCABULARY PANEL to describe the photos. Use a dictionary to help you.

3 **a** 2.1 Listen to four people describing a place. Match each speaker to one of the photos.

Roxanne	☐	Sunee	☐
Juan	☐	Mohammed	☐

b Listen again and complete the sentences with words from A.

1 Roxanne's favourite place is a Chinese ....
2 Juan goes to the .... most weekends.
3 Sunee lives on the .... of Phuket in Thailand. She often goes to the .... to meet friends.
4 Mohammed thinks that the .... can be dangerous, but it's very beautiful, especially in the ....

4 Complete B in the KEY VOCABULARY PANEL. Listen again. Which point of the compass does each speaker mention?

5 **a** Work in groups. Can you remember who said these sentences?

1 'It's a really peaceful place.'
2 *'It's very friendly.'*
3 'This place is unique – there's nowhere quite like it.'
4 'It's noisy and dirty!'

b Read transcript 2.1 on page 162. Underline other adjectives to describe places. Which adjectives describe your hometown?

6 Work in pairs. Discuss the questions.

- Which of the places in the photos do you like the most? Why?
- What is your favourite outdoor place? Why do you like it?

e

f

KEY VOCABULARY

Geography

A Outdoor places

far from everywhere | in a field | in a forest | in a rainforest | in the country | in the desert | in the mountains | near the sea | on an island | on the banks of a river | on the beach | on the coast

B Points of the compass

- Label the compass using *north*, *south*, *east*, *west*.

1 ....

2 ....

3 ....

4 ....

- Match the places on the map to the phrases in the box. (There are more phrases than places).

near the capital | in the centre | in the east | inland | on an island | in the north | in the south | on the west coast

Coimbra is in the centre.

- Where is your hometown? Use the words above to describe exactly where you live.

I live in a small town in the north. It's on the coast, near the capital.

- PRACTISE THE PAST SIMPLE
- TALK ABOUT SURVIVAL STORIES

READING

1 Work in pairs. Look at the photos and newspaper headlines. What do you think is similar about these three stories?

a
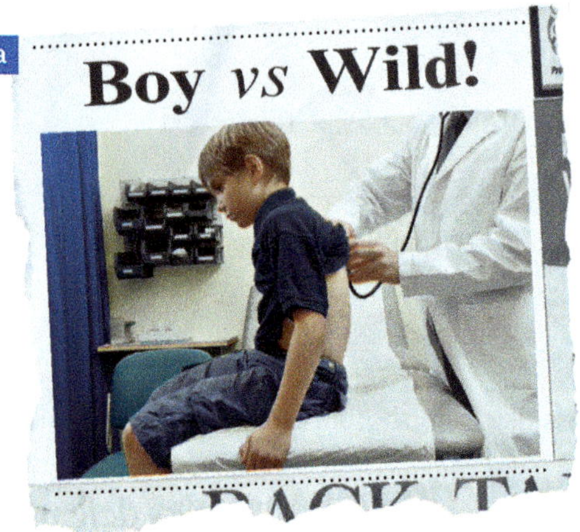

b

c

2 a Read newspaper articles 1–3 and match them to headlines a–c in 1.

b Read the sentences. Are they true or false? Correct the false sentences.

1 Christopher used his mobile phone to call for help.
2 Christopher was walking somewhere cold.
3 Grayson did not have anything to eat.
4 Grayson was wearing something bright.
5 Rory thinks that TV can sometimes be useful.
6 Rory was lost for more time than Christopher and Grayson.

1

A few years ago, Rory and Chiara Maddocks and Rachel Hodson lost their way in a rainforest in central Malaysia. They didn't have any food or drink, and they were tired and scared. The forest was beautiful, but it was dangerous, with many wild animals and rainy weather.
How did the three friends survive? They followed tips from Ray Mears's *Extreme Survival* programme on TV. They walked to a river until they saw the sea. They swam and they tried to find help. Luckily, some boys on a boat rescued them. After two nights in the forest, they were safe.
When he got home, Rory said he wanted to watch more *Extreme Survival*. 'You never know when you might need it!'

2

In 2009, nine-year-old Grayson Wynne spent 18 hours alone in a forest in eastern Utah, USA. He survived – thanks to TV adventurer Bear Grylls.
Grayson and his family were on a camping holiday. On Saturday, Grayson went for a walk by himself. He put some food in his rucksack before he left. But he didn't take a map!
Grayson was a big fan of Bear Grylls's books and TV shows, and he knew what to do. Bear said that it was important to help people to find you, so Grayson left pieces of his yellow jacket on paths and in trees. Rescuers found Grayson after they noticed the yellow material.

3

When Christopher Traverse's snowmobile broke last winter, the Canadian was worried. He didn't know where he was, and he didn't have a mobile phone with him. Luckily, he remembered a TV show called *Survivorman*. As part of the show, a man called Les Stroud stayed in many wild, dangerous places. Christopher decided to use some of Les's ideas. He slept in shelters which he made out of trees, and he drank snow. He got up each day at dawn, and he walked until it grew dark. Four days later, he found a road, and a way home.

3 Find words/phrases in the articles that mean:

1 did not know where they were (3 words)
2 felt unhappy about something bad (1 word)
3 advice, useful ideas (1 words)
4 with no other people (two items: 1 word / 2 words)
5 safe places to sleep (1 word)
6 the beginning of the day (1 word)

4 Work in groups. Discuss the questions.

- Which story did you find the most interesting? Why?
- Are survival television shows popular in your country?
- Would you be good at surviving outdoors? Why/Why not?

GRAMMAR

1 a Work in pairs. Find the sentences in the articles.

1 They **noticed** the yellow material.
2 He **didn't have** a mobile phone with him.
3 How **did** the three friends **survive**?

b Complete 1 and 2 in the GRAMMAR PANEL.

2 Underline the past simple verbs in one of the articles. Which verbs are a) regular? b) irregular?

3 Look at the highlighted words in the articles. Complete 3–7 in the GRAMMAR PANEL.

4 a Look at the photo of Bear Grylls. What do you remember about him from the article?

b Complete the text using the past simple form of the verbs.

Q How (1)*Bear / become* a famous adventurer?

A
- He (2)*climb* Mount Everest aged only 23.
- In 2003, he (3)*go* across the Arctic Ocean. He (4)*not travel* on a big ship, but on a tiny boat!
- Two years later, he (5)*fly* over Angel Falls in Venezuela in a paraglider.

Q What (6)*he / do* on his first show?

A
- On *Man vs Wild*, Bear (7)*sleep* outside in many wild places. He (8)*not stay* in warm hotels!
- He (9)*not take* any food with him. On the show, he (10)*eat* many strange things, like snakes and sheep's eyes!

5 a Think about the last time you visited the countryside. Make questions. Then note your answers.

1 When / go What / weather like
2 Where / go What / place like
3 What / do anything interesting happen

b Work in pairs. Discuss with a partner.

PAST SIMPLE

We use the **past simple** for completed past actions.

(+) *They* ...visited... *wild places.*
(–) *They* (1) .... *any cities.*
(?) *Which countries* (2) .... *they* .... ?

Some verbs have an irregular affirmative form (+).
make → *made*, *do* → *did*, etc.

Time expressions

We often use time words with the past simple, such as:
ago, (3) a...., (4) i...., (5) l........, (6) o...., (7) w........ .

She went there last week. *They left at half past ten.*
He left two hours ago. *We found her on June 9th.*
I lived there in 2003. *It was cold when we left.*

See page 141 for grammar reference and more practice.

PRONUNCIATION: past simple endings

1 a Complete the table with the past simple form of the regular verbs.

Infinitive	Past simple	Infinitive	Past simple
decide	....	stay	....
follow	....	stop	....
need	....	walk	....
notice	....	want	....

b 2.2 Look at the infinitive forms. Which verbs have two syllables? Listen and check.

2 a 2.3 Listen to both the infinitive and the past simple forms. For which three verbs do we pronounce the *-ed* ending as an extra syllable /ɪd/ ? Listen again and repeat.

b Complete the rule.

When the infinitive form of the verb ends in a /....../ or /....../ sound, the *-ed* ending is pronounced as an extra syllable /ɪd/.

3 a Read the sentences. Which past simple endings are pronounced as an extra syllable?

1 We went camping last weekend. It rained and rained. I hated it!
2 I visited my grandparents last Sunday. We sat in the garden and talked about the weather.
3 We went on a long walk. We started at nine and we didn't get back until half past six!

b 2.4 Listen and repeat.

4 Write three sentences about last weekend. Use at least one regular past simple verb in each one.

2.2 CAPTURING THE WILD

- Practise the past continuous & past simple
- Talk about what was happening in the past

a

b

c

d

SPEAKING & LISTENING

1 Work in pairs. Look at the photos. Discuss the questions.

- Where were the photographers when they took the photos?
- How often do you take photos?
- Do you use a camera or your mobile phone? Which do you prefer?

2 Work in pairs. Look at jobs 1–3. Discuss the questions.

1 news photographer
2 wildlife photographer
3 wedding photographer

Which job

- do you think is the most difficult? Why?
- would you like to do the most/least?

3 2.5 Listen to a radio interview with a wildlife photographer. Which three animals in the photos does he talk about?

4 Read the questions. Listen again and circle the answers.

1 When did Steve win the photography competition?
 a this morning
 b a few days ago
 c last year

2 Steve took his winning photo when he was
 a sailing on a river.
 b walking beside a river.
 c sitting next to a river.

3 Steve got his first camera when he was
 a seven.
 b eight.
 c nine.

4 While he was travelling last year, Steve visited
 a Africa.
 b Australia.
 c North America.

5 Steve's favourite animals are
 a lions.
 b snakes.
 c birds.

6 Which animal took Steve's food?
 a a bird
 b a monkey
 c a crocodile

Grammar

1 **a** Read the sentences. Which photos (a–d) is Steve talking about?

1 My girlfriend and I **were travelling** through Bolivia.
2 I **was working** in Africa.

b Look at the verbs in **bold** in 1a. Complete 1 and 2 in the Grammar panel.

2 Read transcript 2.5 on page 162. Find five more examples of the past continuous.

3 **a** What were the animals in photos a–d doing when Steve took the photos?
Write sentences using the verbs in the box.
More than one answer may be possible.

The zebra was running.

chase	climb	jump	run
sit	stand	swim	watch

b Work in pairs. Compare your answers with a partner. Did you use the same verbs?

4 Look at photos e–h. What do you think the photographer was doing at the time?

I think he/she was travelling in a helicopter.

5 Work in pairs. Try to guess what your partner was doing at these times. Ask and answer. Were you right?

What were you doing:
1 ten minutes ago?
2 yesterday evening?
3 last summer?
Were you:
4 studying English this time five years ago?
5 living in the same place in 2000?

e

f

g

h

Past continuous

We use the **past continuous** to talk about an action that was in progress at a specific time in the past.

He was working in Africa at the time.

We form the past continuous with ***was/were*** + verb + ***-ing***.

(+) *It* (1) .... *swimming.*
(–) *It wasn't moving.*
(?) *What* (2) .... *they doing?*

See page 141 for grammar reference and more practice.

Speaking

1 Work in pairs. Look at the photo. Discuss the questions using the words in the box.

have/party	laugh
swim walk	watch

- What was the bull doing just before the photo?
- What were other people doing?
- What do you think happened afterwards?

2 2.6 Listen to a woman talking about what happened. Check your ideas.

■ PRACTISE THE PAST SIMPLE & PAST CONTINUOUS
■ TALK ABOUT MORE THAN ONE ACTION IN THE PAST

a

b

c

d

SPEAKING & VOCABULARY: animals

1 **a** Look at the photos. Can you name the animals? If not, find their names in the box. Use a dictionary to help you.

cat cow deer dog fox giraffe horse lion monkey pig polar bear rabbit sheep snake

b What are the animals doing in each photo? Which situation would worry you most?

2 **a** Match the animal names in 1a to the categories. Use a dictionary to help you. Some animals can go in more than one category.

1 Common pets *rabbit* ....
2 Zoo animals ....
3 Wild animals *rabbit* ....
4 Common farm animals ....

b Can you add at least one more animal to each category?

3 Work in pairs. Discuss the questions with a partner.

- Is there a particular animal that is associated with your country or region?
- If yes, what is it?
- Why is this animal important?

I'm from Wales. Two animals are important in my country. The first is a mythical animal, the dragon – it's on our flag. The second is a sheep – there are more than 20 million sheep in Wales!

LISTENING

1 **a** 2.7 Listen to Jan and Lucia talking about an encounter with animals. Match their conversations to two of photos a–d.

b Listen again. Match the statements to the people, Lucia (L), Jan (J) or both (B).

1 It was the first night of the holiday. *J*
2 It was the last day of the holiday. ....
3 She enjoyed the holiday. ....
4 They went to look at some animals. ....
5 Some animals came to look at them. ....
6 The experience scared her at first. ....
7 The experience made her laugh. ....

2 Check your answers in transcript 2.7 on page 162.

3 **a** Look at the pairs of sentences. Choose the correct option, a or b, for each one.

Conversation 1
1 a The cows were in the campsite.
  b The tent wasn't in the campsite.
2 a The cows sounded human.
  b The cows didn't sound human.
3 a One of the campers opened the door of the tent.
  b One of the cows opened the door of the tent.

Conversation 2
4 a They were driving past a zoo.
  b They were driving through a safari park.
5 a They were following some animals.
  b Some animals were following them.
6 a They chased the monkeys away.
  b Some men chased the monkeys away.

b Listen again and check your answers.

4 Work in pairs. Discuss the questions with a partner. Whose story do you think is

- more interesting? Why?
- more amusing? Why?

Grammar

1 **a** Complete the sentences with the correct endings in the box.

> some monkeys jumped on the car
> took my sunglasses
> Agata opened the door of the tent
> a cow put its head inside the tent

Conversation 1

1 While we **were talking** about what to do, ...

2 She **opened** the door and ....

Conversation 2

3 We **were driving** through a safari park when ....

4 One of the monkeys **climbed** through the window and ....

b Work in pairs. Answer the questions.

1 Look at the verbs in **bold** in 1a. Which are in
   a the past simple?
   b the past continuous?

2 Look at the second verb in each sentence. Which describe
   a an action that happened while the first action was in progress?
   b an action that happened immediately after the first action?

2 Choose the correct options to complete 1–4 in the Grammar panel.

3 Choose the correct form of the verbs to complete the story.

> We [(1)] *walked / were walking* along a quiet country road when we [(2)] *heard / were hearing* a noise in the trees. We [(3)] *stopped / were stopping* and [(4)] *were listening / listened* carefully. Suddenly, a fox [(5)] *jumped / was jumping* into the middle of the road. It [(6)] *carried / was carrying* a bird in its mouth. It [(7)] *looked / was looking* at us, then [(8)] *was turning / turned* and [(9)] *was running / ran* away.

4 **a** Work in pairs. Look at the pictures. Write a short story about what happened.

b 2.8 Listen to Alison talking about her experience. Compare her story with your own. Were there any differences?

5 **a** Work in groups to discuss the questions.

- Have you ever seen an animal in the wild?
- If yes, where were you?
- What were you doing?
- What happened?

b Report the most interesting story to the class.

Past simple & past continuous

We often use the **past continuous** and the **past simple** in the same sentence. This shows that an action happened while a longer action was in progress:

*We **were driving** through a safari park (a) when some monkeys **jumped** on the car (b).*

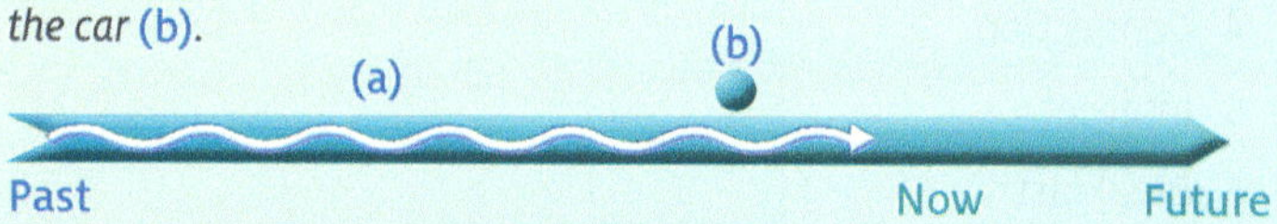

The [(1)] *past continuous / simple* describes the shorter, completed action. The [(2)] *past continuous / simple* describes a longer action that was in progress at the time.

We often use the [(3)] *past continuous / past simple* with ***while***:

*While we **were talking** about what to do, Agata **opened** the door of the tent.*

We can use two verbs in the **past simple** to show that one action followed another:

*Agata **opened** the door (a) and a cow **put** its head in (b).* (= first Agata opened the door and after that, the cow put its head in.)

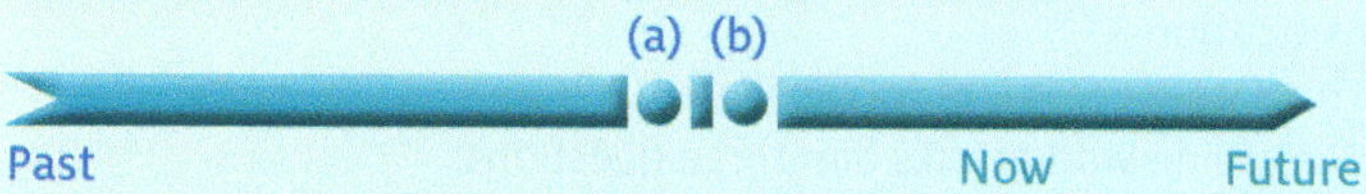

We often use linkers like ***and***, ***then*** and ***so*** with the [(4)] *past continuous / past simple* to introduce the second action.

*So we **put** the tent up quickly, then we **went** to bed.*

See page 141 for grammar reference and more practice.

2.4 FUNCTIONAL LANGUAGE: CHECKING IN

TUNE IN

1 **a** Look at the photos. Where are the people? What is the connection with the title of the lesson?

a

b

b Match the words to the situations in the photos. Some words go with both situations.

	a	b
1 Boarding pass		✓
2 Passport	✓	✓
3 Reference number		
4 Connection		
5 Internet		
6 Breakfast		
7 Boarding gate		
8 Suite		
9 Bags		

2 **a** 2.9 Listen to two conversations. Match them to the photos in 1a. <u>Underline</u> the words you hear in 1b.

b Listen again. Mark the statements true (T) or false (F). Correct the false statements.

Conversation 1
1 The passenger is late for his flight.
2 The airline worker asks him three questions.
3 They don't know how long the delay is.

Conversation 2
1 The couple have booked the room for two nights.
2 The room price doesn't include breakfast.
3 The receptionist has given the guests a better room.

FOCUS ON LANGUAGE

3 **a** Match extracts 1–9 from the conversations to people a–c.

a airline worker b hotel receptionist c hotel guest

1 Is breakfast included?
2 Here's a free pass to our business lounge.
3 Can I check in, please?
4 I'm afraid there's a delay to your flight.
5 I'm pleased to tell you, you have a suite!
6 I'm afraid there's an extra cost for internet. Here are the details.
7 How many bags do you want to check in?
8 Do you have your booking reference number?
9 Can I have your passports, please?

b Match responses a–i to extracts 1–9.

a Just this one.
b Yes, of course, here they are.
c Yes, here it is, we booked online.
d Let me check, sir...
e Of course, do you have your booking reference number?
f Oh, that's a shame.
g Oh, that's a surprise. Thanks very much.
h Oh, that's great... thank you!
i Oh dear... how long is it?

4 Listen again and check.

"Intonation: sounding surprised and disappointed"

2.10 Look again at the last four responses in 3b. Which speakers are a) happy? b) unhappy?

Listen to the four responses. What do you notice about the intonation? When does it a) go up? b) go down?

Practise saying the responses sounding surprised or disappointed.

OVER TO YOU

5 **a** Work in pairs. Act out the first situation (at an airport check-in desk). Student A, turn to page 158. Student B, turn to page 160.

b Act out the second situation (at a hotel reception). Student A, turn to page 158. Student B, turn to page 160.

TUNE IN

1 Work in pairs. Look at the photos on a travel website. Discuss the questions.

1 Where did the woman go on holiday?
2 What did she do on holiday?
3 Do you think she enjoyed it? Why?

2 Quickly read the holiday review and check your answers to 1.

3 The website has a 'rate this review' feature, where readers decide how useful a review is. How would you rate this review? Why?

Holiday company: Wild Travel
Reviewer: Sally Castle

Rate this review:

very useful ☆☆☆☆☆
quite useful ☆☆☆
not useful ☆

HOLIDAY REVIEW

a When we booked our holiday, my husband and I were really excited. We are both quite adventurous people, so trekking on the island of Borneo seemed like our dream holiday. Unfortunately, it was more like a nightmare!

b We travelled in summer, so we were expecting hot, sunny weather. But when we arrived at the airport, it was raining. It rained for fourteen days! We walked for more than 10 kilometres every day, but we didn't see any interesting wildlife – only dangerous snakes! Our tour guide, Azman, wasn't very reliable. On the first day, he was two hours late. Then he lost our map while we were following a river. We were walking until midnight that night!

c By the end of the holiday, we were tired and fed up. Borneo was beautiful. But the best part of our holiday was going home!

PREPARE FOR TASK

4 Match paragraphs a–c to descriptions 1–3.

1 giving a conclusion
2 setting the scene
3 describing what happened

5 Read the review again. Find and <u>underline</u> two examples of

1 past tenses
2 time expressions
3 adjectives
4 linkers

TASK

6 Imagine you are going to write about a holiday experience for the website. Choose one of the following:

- an amazing holiday experience
- a terrible holiday experience

7 Think of an experience to describe. You can use your own ideas, or describe an experience from the news or TV. Answer the questions in the paragraph plan.

Paragraph	*Content ideas*
1	*Where did you go on holiday? When did you go? Who did you go with?*
2	*What happened on the holiday? Why was it good/bad?*
3	*How did you feel after the holiday?*

8 Now write a short description of your holiday experience. Remember to:
1 follow the paragraph plan in 7. 2 use a variety of language as in 5.

REPORT BACK

9 **a** Compare your reviews in groups.

b What are the two most interesting things about each story?

10 Decide as a group which was your favourite holiday review. Why?

➜ Go to Review A, Unit 2, p. 35

3 ICONS

a

b

c

e

f

g

1 **a** Work in groups. Look at the photos. Do you recognise the landmarks? Where are they?

b 3.1 Listen to two radio presenters talking about the landmarks. Check your answers to a and answer the questions.

1 What are the Seven Wonders of the Modern World?
2 When was the list announced?
3 Which photo is not one of the seven? Why?

2 Work in groups. Discuss the questions.

- Have you ever visited any of the landmarks?
- If yes, when? What was your impression?
- If no, which one would you most like to visit? Why?

3 Work in pairs. Complete A and B in the KEY VOCABULARY PANEL. What are the most famous landmarks in your country? Do you know why and when they were built?

4 **a** 3.2 Listen to short extracts from audio guides for tourists at two of these landmarks. Which landmarks are they describing?

b Listen again and complete the extracts.

1 It is almost .... metres tall – one of the tallest sculptures ever made of the Christ figure.
2 A .... **engineer**, Heitor da Silva Costa, drew up the **design**s for the statue.
3 It took the .... **sculptor** Paul Landowski .... years to build it.
4 It was designed by a team of local **architect**s in the traditional style of .... architecture of the time.
5 It took .... years to complete.

d

h

Key vocabulary

Landmarks

A Types of landmarks

- Match words from the box to the photos. Which don't match any of the photos?

arena bridge city palace ruins
sculpture statue temple tower wall

B Reasons for building landmarks

- Match the reasons for building the landmarks to photos a–h. Check your answers on page 158.
  - as **a defence** against invasion
  - **in memory of** a loved one
  - **to hold** competitions
  - **to bury** the dead
  - **to protect** an important source of water
  - as a religious **monument**
  - as a **capital city**
  - for an **emperor**

C Word families

What it is	Person who does it
architecture	....
building	builder
....	designer
engineering	....
sculpture	....

- 3.3 Listen to the words and mark the stress. Listen again and repeat.

5 Work in pairs. Do you know anything else about these two landmarks or any of the others in the photos? Share your information with the class.

6 Use the words in **bold** in 4b to complete C in the Key vocabulary panel.

7 a Work in groups. Think of a landmark in your country. Write a short description for a tourist audio guide. Use the Key vocabulary panel and include information about

- where it is.
- what it looks like.
- when and why it was built.
- anything else you know about it.

b Read your description to the class without giving the name of the landmark. Can they guess what it is?

- PRACTISE RELATIVE CLAUSES
- TALK ABOUT FAMOUS BUILDINGS

a

b

c

d

e

f

g

READING

1 Work in pairs. Look at photos a–i of the Taj Mahal. Which is the original building? What are the others? Describe them to your partner.

2 Look at the title of the article. What do you think it will say about the Taj Mahal?

- There are so many imitations that there's no reason to see the real thing.
- There are so many imitations that you have to see the real thing.
- We cannot tell the difference between real things and imitations any more.

3 Read the article and check your answer to 2. Underline the parts of the article that refer to photos a–i and match them to the photos.

4 a Read the article again. Correct the false sentences.

1 There is no connection between the Mona Lisa and the Taj Mahal.
2 Westerners see the building as being very familiar.
3 The Taj Mahal casino in Atlantic City is an exact copy of the original building.
4 Many Chinese restaurants in the world are called the Taj Mahal.
5 You can't get much Taj Mahal merchandising.
6 You realise that the real Taj Mahal is different as soon as you see it.

b After reading the article, are you more or less interested in visiting the Taj Mahal? Why/Why not?

Will the REAL Taj Mahal please stand up?

Writer Salman Rushdie said that the Taj Mahal sits at the top of the West's shortlist of images of the Exotic and Timeless Orient. Like the Mona Lisa, mass reproduction has sterilised it.

The fact is, there are fake Taj Mahals all over the world. The most famous is in Shenzen, China, in the Window of the World theme park. Then there is Donald Trump's luxury Taj Mahal casino in Atlantic City that uses the original building for exotic inspiration. But the building which has caused most controversy is an exact copy made in Bangladesh. Indian authorities are angry with Ahsanullah Moni, a millionaire film maker, who thought up the replica. However, Moni has been quick to defend the building: Everyone dreams about seeing the Taj Mahal, but very few Bangladeshis can make the trip as it's too expensive.

But it's not just the building itself. There are lots of Indian curry restaurants which are called the Taj Mahal and use it as their logo. Children can build Lego models of it, you can get T-shirts and buy posters and, of course, take your own photos.

That's why, at the moment when you're standing in front of it, you can't believe it is real. And this is why you have to see the original, in the place where it truly stands in Agra, India. As Rushdie said, the beauty of beautiful things can still transcend imitations... And the Taj Mahal is a lovely thing, perhaps the loveliest of things.

h

i

Grammar

1 **a** Work in pairs. Cover the Taj Mahal article. Match the two parts of the sentences.

1 There are lots of Indian curry restaurants
2 Indian authorities are angry with a millionaire film maker
3 There is the Taj Mahal casino in Atlantic City

a **which** are called the Taj Mahal.
b **that** uses the original building for exotic inspiration.
c **who** thought up the replica.

b Check your answers in the article.

2 What do the second half of the sentences (a–c) add to the first half (1–3)? Complete 1–4 in the GRAMMAR PANEL.

3 **a** Look at the sentences. Replace *that* with either *who* or *which*.

1 The Taj Mahal is one of the buildings that I'd most like to visit in the world.
2 I've never met anybody that has been to the Taj Mahal.
3 I hate buildings that are just imitations of the original.
4 I know the place that most people in the world want to go to.

b Work in pairs. Which ones are true for you? Change the ones which are not true. Compare your answers with your partner.

Relative clauses

Look at these sentences.

There are lots of Indian curry restaurants. They are called the Taj Mahal.

There are lots of Indian curry restaurants which are called the Taj Mahal.

When we join two sentences together in this way, the first part is the **main** clause and the other part is the **relative** clause.

There are lots of Indian curry restaurants is the (1) .... clause.

which are called the Taj Mahal. is the (2) .... clause.

We use *who*, *which* and *that* to link the two clauses. They replace nouns or pronouns in the original sentences.

This is the photo. I took it at the Taj Mahal. → *This is the photo* ***that*** *I took at the Taj Mahal.*

This is the man. He built the casino. → *This is the man* ***who*** *built the casino.*

We use (3) .... or *that* to refer to things.

We use (4) .... or *that* to refer to people.

See page 142 for grammar reference and more practice.

Listening & Speaking

1 Look at the photo. Guess who and where the people are.

2 **a** 3.4 Listen and check your answers. Identify the people in the photo.

b Listen again and complete the sentences.

This is the Alhambra taken from the Plaza San Nicolas, (1) .... is in the Albaicín, the Arab quarter. This is the place where I was happiest on my trip to Europe last year. There were five of us on that trip. You can see David sitting on the left, and next to him, Rod is playing the guitar. That's the guitar (2) .... he bought in Granada. In fact, he learned to play on that trip! But I love the photo because Neil looks so silly. He's the one (3) .... is taking a picture of the wrong thing! I'm not there, of course; I'm the one (4) .... took the photo.

- PRACTISE ARTICLES
- DISCUSS ICONS & GESTURES

READING

1 Work in groups. Look at icons a–k and answer the questions.

1. What do these icons mean and where do you see them?
2. Can you think of other icons we use and recognise in different parts of the world?

2 Read the blog post. Which icon is it discussing?

ARTICLES | ABOUT | CONTRIBUTE | SUBSCRIBE | CONTACT

ICON DESIGN

There are lots of icons used in technology that are clever and creative. I like the house icon on the internet to represent a 'homepage'. It looks just like the houses that children draw! I like the bin, too – that's the place where you put the things you don't want. It's a very clear icon. The symbols and the icons that Messenger, Twitter and Facebook use are also fine because they're attractive and everyone recognises them. But there is one icon which just doesn't work these days: the floppy disk icon for 'save'.

Computers don't use floppy disks anymore. They stopped using them in 2002! Young people don't know what they are. I think they should design a new icon. There must be an icon out there that's more modern. Here are some ideas I came up with. What do you think? Which do you like best? Or do you have a better idea?

3 **a** Read the blog post again. Are the sentences true or false?

1. The writer likes some icons used in technology.
2. The last new computers to use floppy disks were in 2002.
3. Children know what a floppy disk is.
4. The writer wants a new icon for 'save'.

b Do you agree with the blog post? Why/Why not?

4 **a** Look at the new icons for 'save'. Which do you like best? Why? Can you think of any others? Draw your own version.

b Compare with other groups. Who has the best one?

GRAMMAR

1 **a** Work in pairs. Cover the text in READING 2. Complete the sentences with the words in the box.

bin children floppy disks
icon (x2) internet technology

1. There are lots of icons used in .... that are clever and creative.
2. I like the house icon on the .... to represent a 'homepage'.
3. It looks just like the houses that .... draw!
4. I like the .... , too – that's the place where you put things you don't want.
5. Computers don't use .... anymore.
6. I think they should design a new ....
7. There must be an .... out there that's more modern.

b Check your answers in the text.

2 **a** Underline all the examples of *a/an* and *the* in the sentences in 1a. Which nouns do they refer to? Can you find six nouns that don't have an article?

b Complete 1–6 in the GRAMMAR PANEL with examples from 1a.

3 Read the reply to the blog post. Complete it with *a/an*, *the* or no article.

> I agree with you. (1) .... icon for 'save' is ridiculous. I have (2) .... 12-year-old child and I asked her if she knew what it was. She said it was (3) .... blue square! If we want to use (4) .... icons, not (5) .... words, then we must use (6) .... icons that everyone recognises.

4 Work in pairs. Talk about an icon or logo that you like or dislike. Complete the sentences.

1 I like/don't like the icon/logo for...
2 Icons are a good form of communication because...
3 I think tattoos are interesting icons. The most common tattoos are...
4 Gestures can also be icons. For example, we have a gesture here which...

ARTICLES: *A/AN*, *THE*, NO ARTICLE

A/an

We use *a/an* to talk about a person or thing in a general way.

We need ***a*** *new icon.* (we don't know which specific icon)

(1) ....

Use *a* and *an* with singular countable nouns.

Use *a* before a consonant sound and *an* before a vowel sound.

a (2) ...., *an* (3) ....

The

We use *the* to talk about a specific person or thing.

The ***houses*** *that children draw.*

(4) ....

We also use *the* when there is only one example in our world or experience.

the moon, the world, (5) ....

No article

We can't use *a/an* with uncountable nouns or plural nouns.

If we want to talk about uncountable or plural nouns in a general way, we don't use an article.

There are lots of icons (NOT ~~the~~ *icons*) *in technology* (NOT ~~the~~ *technology*)

(6) ....

See page 142 for grammar reference and more practice.

PRONUNCIATION: *the & a*

1 **a** Complete the phrases with *a* or *an*.

.... unusual icon	.... new icon
.... interesting icon	.... international gesture
.... confusing gesture	.... universal gesture
.... Asian icon	.... European gesture

b 3.5 Listen and check.

2 Look at the phrases in 1a again. Complete the rules using *a* or *an*.

1 We use .... before a consonant sound.
2 We use .... before a vowel sound.

Some words that start with a vowel are pronounced with a semi-vowel sound, e.g. /j/: *universal, university, European*

3 We use .... before a word that starts with /j/.

3 **a** 3.6 Complete the sentences with *a* or *an*. Listen to the pronunciation of *a/an*. Is it weak or strong?

1 I'm .... only child.
2 My brother's .... university student.
3 My eyes are .... unusual colour.
4 I drive .... European car.

b Listen again and repeat.

SPEAKING

1 **a** Look at the photos. What do the gestures mean?

b 3.7 Listen and match the speakers to the photos.

2 What gestures do you use to indicate these ideas?

- how tall someone is
- eating
- I don't know
- money
- drinking
- what time is it?

LISTENING & VOCABULARY: cultural icons

1 **a** Read the definition.

> **cultural icon** A *cultural icon* can be an image, a logo, picture, name, face, person or building that people recognise immediately. It usually represents an object or concept with great meaning to a large cultural group.

b Work in pairs. Look at the photos of 'cultural icons'. Do you agree with the definition? Why/Why not?

2 **a** 3.8 Listen to three people giving an opinion about some of the icons above. Which icons do they mention? What do they think of them?

b Match the speakers to the points they make.

1 It represents a particular country.
2 It's a cultural icon for some parts of the world.
3 It can show that people have money or are important.

3 **a** Look at the adjectives. Which speaker uses these adjectives? Listen again to check.

> familiar famous iconic
> legendary popular well-known

b Rank the words in order of fame.

MOST FAMOUS 1 .... 2 .... 3 ....
4 .... 5 .... 6 .... LEAST FAMOUS

4 Look at the nouns which can refer to famous people. Which can also be used to refer to objects?

> a celebrity a household name an icon
> a legend a (super)star

5 **a** Complete the sentences using words from 4.

1 Nelson Mandela is ....
2 Che Guevara is ....
3 Levi's is ....
4 Rubik's Cube is ....
5 James Bond is ....
6 Mickey Mouse is ....

b Work in pairs. Compare your ideas with your partner. Do you have similar answers?

6 Work in pairs. In your country or culture, which people or things are iconic? Why?

7 **a** Work in groups. Who and what do you think are global cultural icons? Make a list of six people or objects.

b Report back to the class with your list. Compare your list with other groups.

Reading

1 **a** You are going to read about Bob Marley. Make a list of things you know already about him.

b Now read and check. Are the things you wrote mentioned in the article? Write down at least one thing that you did not know about him.

The Legend of Bob Marley

Few singers have had the influence on music that Bob Marley has had. He was born in a small village in Jamaica as Nesta Robert Marley in 1945 to a young black mother and an older white father.

In 1963, Bob Marley formed a group, who became the famous Wailers. In 1966, Marley became a member of the Rastafarian movement, and started to wear his famous <u>dreadlocks</u> hairstyle. Their first album came out in 1973, but it was in 1975 that Marley became an international star with his first hit outside Jamaica, '<u>No Woman, No Cry</u>'. Marley was suddenly a celebrity.

Marley was important around the world as a musician, but in Jamaica he was more than just a singer – he was a huge cultural icon. Some said he was even more important than the Jamaican government in the 1970s. On December 5, 1976, Marley was going to give a free 'Smile Jamaica' concert, to help to unite the people of his country. Just before the concert, gunmen attacked Bob Marley and his friends. He was injured, but he amazed the crowd of 80,000 people when he appeared to play at the concert two days later. He really seemed to be superhuman, and this helped to make him the legend that he is today.

In 1977, doctors found that Marley had cancer, and he died on 11 May 1981 at the age of 36. Bob Marley's music lives on and he has become the symbol of reggae music all over the world.

2 **a** Read the article again and complete this timeline about Bob Marley's life.

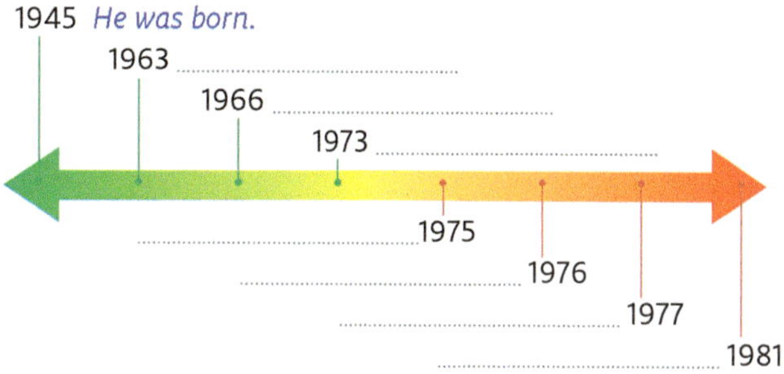

b Which do you think was the most important event in his life and why?

3 **a** Imagine you want to describe Bob Marley to someone who doesn't know him. Complete the sentences.

Bob Marley is the person who ....
He is famous for ....
What people don't know is that he ....

b Work in pairs. Compare your sentences.

4 Do you, or any of your friends, listen to Bob Marley's music? Is reggae popular in your country?

Listening

1 Work in pairs. Look at the photos. Do you know anything about these iconic fictional characters?

2 **a** 3.9 Listen to two people discussing the characters. Who does Karina like? Who does Simon like?

b Listen again. Complete the sentences with Karina (K) or Simon (S).

1 .... thinks *The Simpsons* is about serious things.
2 .... likes shows using real actors.
3 .... thinks *House* is not a perfect character.
4 .... thinks *The Simpsons* makes you think and laugh.
5 .... says Dr House and Homer Simpson are both unreal.

3 Do you agree with Karina and Simon? Are there other fictional characters that you consider to be 'cultural icons'? Why?

4 **a** Work in groups. Choose four iconic characters, real or fictional, to invite to a party.

I'd like to invite... because...

b Compare your list with another group. Who has the most interesting party?

3.4 FUNCTIONAL LANGUAGE: EXPRESSING PREFERENCE

TUNE IN

1 Look at the photos of laptop 'skins'. Do you think they are a good idea? Which one do you like best?

2 3.10 Listen to four people talking about laptop skins. Which one do they prefer?

Jake: .... Carly: .... Dave: .... Sal: ....

3 Listen again. Which of the opinions is not mentioned?

1 Nature scenes are not interesting.
2 A laptop skin needs to say something about the owner.
3 Laptop skins help to keep a laptop clean.
4 A laptop skin is better if it's not in fashion.
5 A laptop skin should show your interests.
6 It's better to have your own design.
7 Laptop skins are not necessary at all.

FOCUS ON LANGUAGE

4 Listen again and complete the sentences.

1 Which is your .... , Jake?
2 Personally, I .... the ones that show beautiful scenery.
3 I .... have one that says something about me and who I am.
4 I .... something more classic, like a piece of art.
5 I .... to have something that shows one of my hobbies or interests.
6 Wouldn't .... to have a custom design?

NOTICE *PERSONALLY*

We use *personally* to emphasise that what you are saying is your personal opinion.
Personally, I prefer laptops to desktop computers.

5 Complete the table of ways to ask about and express preferences. Use your answers from 4 to help you.

Asking about preferences	Expressing preferences
• What's your .... ?	• I (much) ....
• Which is better?	• I'd (much) prefer...
• Which do you .... ?	• I'd (much) ....
• Would(n't) it be .... to... ?	• I like .... best (of all).
	• I like .... better than ....

Intonation: adding emphasis

3.11 Listen and underline the word which adds emphasis in these sentences.

1 *I'd rather have something modern.*
2 *I'd much rather have something modern.*
3 *I'd prefer a piece of art.*
4 *I'd much prefer a piece of art.*

Practise saying the sentences with the same emphasis.

6 Work in groups. Which laptop skin would you prefer? Why?

OVER TO YOU

7 Turn to pages 158–159. Imagine you want to choose a template for a blog about your English class. Which of the five templates would you prefer? Discuss with your group. Consider

- design
- colours
- style
- use of images

8 Compare your choice with other groups and choose one for the whole class.

TUNE IN

1 a Work in groups. Look at the logos. What do they say about the companies that they represent?

b Which of the values do the logos suggest about the company?

active creative dynamic exciting fast
fun modern reliable serious traditional

PREPARE FOR TASK

2 a Read the article about designing a good logo. Do the logos in 1 have these features? Complete the table with a tick (✓) or a cross (✗).

Logos are the icons of your business. A logo is a visual icon that identifies a company or product. Logos are very important and can bring success or failure, so you must understand the qualities of good logo design. Here are four easy points to remember:

1 Make an impact – attract attention and make people look at it.
2 Keep it simple.
3 Limit the colours to a maximum of three to keep printing costs low.
4 Represent the company. For example, if it's a serious company, the logo should be serious.

	1	2	3	4
Close Up Photography				
Circumference Travel				
Eden & Lithgow				
Happy Days Nursery				
Creature Comforts				
Hayes & Co				

b Compare in groups. Did you agree on all of the logos?

3 Which logo did you like best and why? Do you think you could improve any of the logos?

TASK

4 Work in groups. Think of a company and a company name. Complete the table about your company.

Name	
Product or service	
Values of the company	
Logo	

5 Design a logo to represent the company. Use 2a to help you.

REPORT BACK

6 Present your logo to the class. Explain about your company using the table in 4.

7 Listen to the presentations. Does the logo follow the four points in 2a? What do you think about the company? Which logo and company is your favourite?

→ Go to Review A, Unit 3, p. 36 → Go to Writing bank 2, p. 153

VOCABULARY

Languages & countries

1 Work in pairs. Answer the questions.

1 Name four countries where English is an official language, but is not a language people speak as a mother tongue.
2 Name four countries where there are lots of bilingual people.

2 Work in groups. Which languages do you speak fluently? How many languages does your group speak in total?

Free time

3 a R1 Look at the photos. Listen and answer the questions.

1 Where are the people from and what languages do they speak?
2 What do they do?
3 What do they do in their free time?

a

b

b Listen again and compare your answers.

Communication

4 Correct the mistakes in **bold**.

Hannah knew that Joe was not (1) **telling truth**. He talked for ten minutes, but she stopped (2) **listening him**. 'You're (3) **telling lie!**' she said finally. He (4) **told she** that he was leaving and he stopped (5) **talking her**. After he left, she sent a text message (6) **at** her friend, but she couldn't think about anything except Joe. She needed to (7) **talk about** him, so she called his mobile.

GRAMMAR

Present simple & present continuous

1 a Complete the sentences with the correct form of the verbs.

1 At the moment I .... *(learn)* French.
2 I .... *(want)* to go to the USA on holiday.
3 I .... *(not eat)* fruit, because I .... *(not like)* it.
4 I .... *(not live)* in my hometown at the moment.

b Work in pairs. Are the sentences in 1a true about you? Compare your answers with your partner.

Questions

2 a Write the words in the correct order.

1 do do you What weekend the at ?
2 live you parents Do with your ?
3 moment What you studying the are at ?
4 work Who with do you ?
5 saw last film What the was you ?
6 like Did it you ?

b Work in groups of three. Ask and answer the questions.

3 a Write one question you would like to ask students in your class.

b Ask students your question and make a note of the answers. Report back to the rest of the class.

FUNCTIONAL LANGUAGE

Checking understanding

1 Complete the questions using the words in the box.

call repeat say (x2)

1 Can you .... it again, please?
2 What did you .... ?
3 Can you .... that, please?
4 What do you .... this in English?

2 a Work in pairs. Think of a reply to each question in 1 and write it down.

b Ask and answer the questions.

LOOKING BACK

- What is easy about learning English? What is difficult?
- Which activity or lesson in this unit did you enjoy most? Why?
- Write down three new things you can say about yourself.

VOCABULARY

Geography

1 Complete the words.

1 Not f........ from means 'near'.
2 A f.................... is a place with lots of trees.
3 A place on the c................ is near the sea.
4 The c.................... of Spain is Madrid.
5 In the c.................... means 'in the middle'.
6 Great Britain, Iceland and Cuba are all i.................... .

2 **a** Use two of the words in 1 to describe two different places in your country.

b Describe your favourite part of the country to your partner. Why do you like it?

Animals

3 **a** Name animals 1–8.

1 .... 2 .... 3 .... 4 ....
5 .... 6 .... 7 .... 8 ....

a .... b .... c .... d ....

b Label each pair of animals a–d using the categories in the box. Can you name any more animals in each category?

zoo animals	wild animals
common pets	common farm animals

4 Is there a particular animal which is important/significant to you? If yes, why is it important?

GRAMMAR

Past simple

1 **a** Complete the sentences with the correct form of the verbs.

1 I .... *(watch)* a TV nature documentary last night.
2 I .... *(do)* something to help the environment yesterday.
3 I .... *(not be)* interested in nature when I was young.
4 I .... *(not visit)* the countryside last year.
5 I .... *(have)* a pet when I was a child.
6 I .... *(not travel)* anywhere on holiday last summer.

b Work in pairs. Are the sentences true for your partner? Take turns to ask and answer questions.

Did you watch a TV nature documentary last night?

Yes, I saw a programme about wildlife in Africa. It was really interesting!

Past continuous & past simple

2 Complete the sentences with the correct form of the verbs.

1 While he .... *(swim)*, he .... *(see)* a crocodile.
2 We .... *(cook)* dinner on a fire when they .... *(find)* us.
3 It .... *(not rain)* in the forest when we .... *(arrive)*.
4 I .... *(walk)* along the path when I .... *(stand)* on a snake!
5 What .... *(you / eat)* while you .... *(wait)* for the rescue team?

FUNCTIONAL LANGUAGE

Checking in

1 **a** Complete the conversations.

1
A How many bags do you want to .... in?
B Just these two, please.

2
A Do you have your .... reference number?
B Yes, here it is... GB458Q.

3
A I'm afraid breakfast isn't included. There's an extra .... of $10.
B Oh, that's a shame.

b R2 Listen and check.

2 Work in pairs. Look at the picture and act out the conversation.

LOOKING BACK

- Which story in this unit did you find the most interesting? Why?
- How many irregular past tenses can you remember?
- Think of three interesting things that happened to you recently. Can you describe what happened?

VOCABULARY

Landmarks

1 a Name as many different types of landmarks as you can.

b Work in pairs. Describe a landmark from your town or country.

2 Find out how many people in your class have visited a famous landmark. What is that landmark and where is it?

Word families

3 a Write the name of the person who does each thing.

1 architecture
2 engineering
3 sculpture
4 design

b Work in groups. Do you know a person who does each thing in a?

Cultural icons

4 a Name five celebrities in your country. Are any of them icons? If yes, why?

b Work in pairs. Tell your partner about the celebrities. Does he/she know them? Does he/she think they are icons?

GRAMMAR

Relative clauses

1 a Choose five items from this unit. Write a definition for each item using *who*, *which* or *that*.

b Work in pairs. Read your definitions to your partner. He/she must guess what they are.

Articles: *a/an*, *the*, no article

2 a Complete the text with definite articles, indefinite articles or no article.

(1) .... mobile phone case is (2) .... good way to protect your mobile phone. (3) .... case you choose depends on (4) .... type of phone you have and what you want to say about yourself. If you choose (5) .... bright colour you are (6) .... outgoing person. If you choose (7) .... dark colour you are (8) .... shy person. So (9) .... mobile phone cases are very important accessories.

b Do you agree with the text? What kind of mobile phone cover do you have? What do you think it says about you?

FUNCTIONAL LANGUAGE

Expressing preference

1 a Match the questions to the answers.

1 Who's your favourite actor?
2 Do you prefer classic or modern art?
3 Which do you prefer?
4 Wouldn't it be better to see the Eiffel Tower first?

a I'd prefer to do that later.
b I like Cate Blanchett best of all.
c I usually like modern art better.
d I'd much rather have this one.

b R3 Listen and check.

2 Work in groups. Discuss your preferences for

1 places to go at the weekend.
2 things to do on your birthday.
3 programmes to watch on TV.
4 food to eat for breakfast.

LOOKING BACK

- Think of three things you learned in this unit.
- Is there anything you want to look at again?
- Tell a partner three preferences you have.

LISTENING

1 R4 Listen to three people introducing themselves on *English Chat*, an online chatroom. Complete their profiles.

Name: Xian
Country: (1) ....
Languages: (2) ....
Started learning English (when?): (3) ....

Name: Natasha
Country: (4) ....
Languages: (5) ....
Started learning English (when?): (6) ....

Name: Tati
Country: (7) ....
Languages: (8) ....
Started learning English (when?): (9) ....

2 a Work in pairs. Look at these 'key words' from the listening. What do you remember about them?

1 Violin
2 Restaurant
3 India
4 The USA
5 Computer games
6 Sister

b Listen again and check.

3 Work in pairs. Discuss the questions.

- Do you write down key words when you listen?
- Can you think of any more listening tips?

READING

4 a Read the description of a good listener. Do you think the *English Chat* moderator was a good listener? Why/Why not?

When someone is speaking, a good listener:
- asks questions if he/she doesn't understand something.
- asks questions to find out more information.
- sounds interested.
- is always polite.

b Work in pairs. Can you think of one more idea to add to the list?

SPEAKING

5 a Work in pairs. Take turns to be Student A and Student B.
Student A, you are a new member of *English Chat*. Introduce yourself to the group. Say four things about yourself.
Student B, you are the chatroom moderator. Welcome Student A to the chatroom, and remember to be a 'good listener'.

b What was the most interesting thing you learnt about your partner?

QUICK CHECK

Complete the checklist below.

Can you...	Yes, I can.	Yes, more or less.	I need to look again.
1 name ten countries and ten languages?	☐	☐	☐
2 talk about your hobbies and interests?	☐	☐	☐
3 talk about what is happening right now?	☐	☐	☐
4 describe places?	☐	☐	☐
5 talk about what you do on holiday?	☐	☐	☐
6 talk about things that happened in the past?	☐	☐	☐
7 describe an interesting building?	☐	☐	☐
8 talk about your preferences?	☐	☐	☐

Compare your answers with a partner.
- What else do you know now after studying units 1–3?
- Do you need to look again at any of the sections?
- Do you need any extra help from your teacher?

4 AGES AND CHANGES

1 Work in pairs. Look at the photos. How old are the people in each photo? What are they celebrating?

2 a 4.1 Listen and check. Match extracts 1–3 to photos a–c.

b What one thing do all three celebrations have in common?

3 Work in groups. Discuss the questions.

- How do young people in your country celebrate their 'coming of age'?
- What was the last birthday party you went to? Whose birthday was it? How and where did you celebrate it?
- How many weddings have you been to? Do you like weddings? Why/Why not?

4 a Work in pairs. Order the words in A in the KEY VOCABULARY PANEL from the youngest to the oldest. What age, more or less, does each category cover?

baby – 0 to 2 years

b Work in groups. Discuss the questions.

- Do you know someone in each age category? How do you know them? Do you spend a lot of time together? What do you usually do together?
- Do you think it's possible to say which is the 'best time' of your life? Why/Why not?

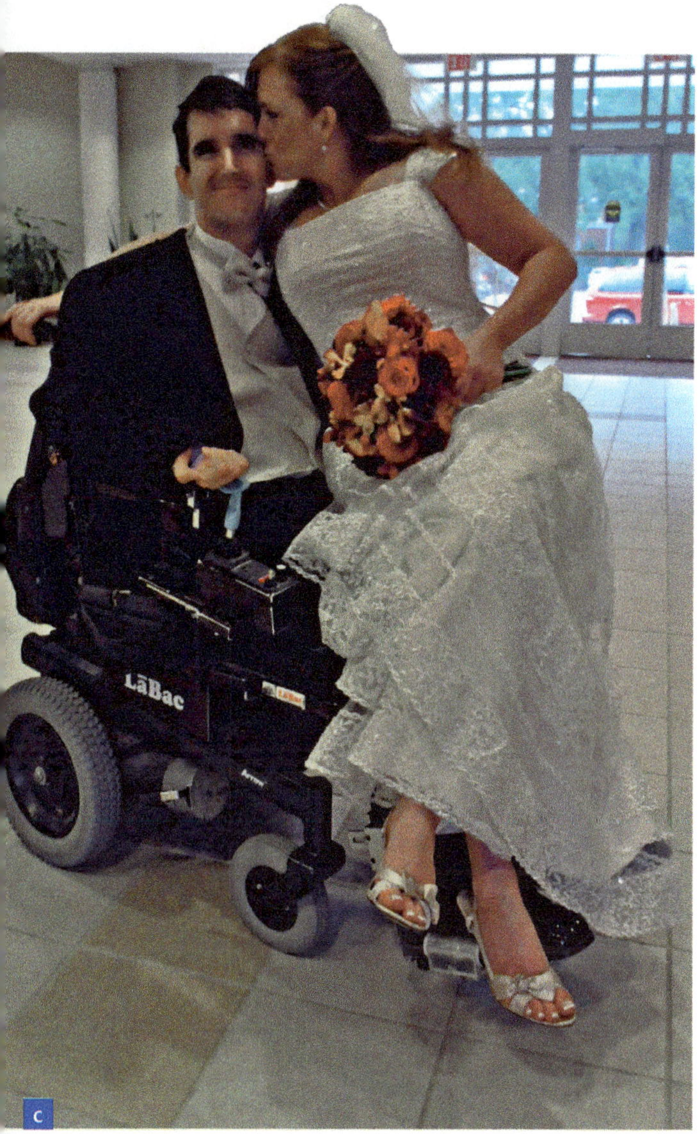

c

KEY VOCABULARY

Life stages

A Ages

adult baby child middle-aged person
pensioner teenager young adult

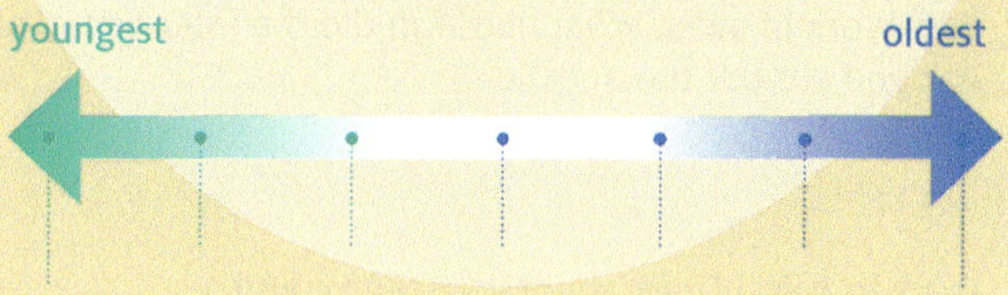

B Stages

- be born
- learn to walk and talk
- become independent
- come of age
- fall in love
- finish school
- get a job
- get divorced
- get married
- go to school for the first time
- go to university
- have children
- leave home
- learn to drive a car
- retire
- vote
- die

NOTICE *GET*

We can use *get* with nouns to talk about something which somebody gives to you, or something you obtain: *He got a job. She got a new car.*
We can use *get* with adjectives to mean *become*.
They got married. They got divorced. NOT ~~They married.~~

5 **a** Work in pairs. Look at B in the KEY VOCABULARY PANEL. Which age/ages do you associate with each stage? Can you think of other stages to add to the list?

b Work in small groups. Discuss the questions.

- How many of the stages have you done?
- How old were you when you did them?
- What, if possible, do you remember about them?

6 **a** People don't always do the stages in the same order. Do you know someone who's done them in an unusual order? Tell your group about that person.

My sister went to university after she got married.

b Share your stories with the class. Whose story was the most unusual?

- PRACTISE THE PRESENT PERFECT
- DISCUSS ACTIVITIES & HOBBIES

SPEAKING & VOCABULARY: activities

1 Work in pairs. Look at photos a–f. What are the people doing? Is there anything unusual about them?

2 **a** Look at the photos again. Complete the activities with *do*, *go* and *play*.

b 4.2 Listen and check.

3 Work in pairs. What question did the interviewer ask? Ask and answer the question.

a .... karate

b .... fishing

d .... golf

f .... skateboardin

READING

1 Work in pairs. Think about your own country. Which hobbies are usually more popular with

- young people?
- old people?
- young and old people?

2 Read the article and answer the questions.

1 What are Ela and Marco's main hobbies?
2 What other hobbies can you find?

3 **a** Read the article again. Decide if these sentences are true or false.

1 Ela only recently started getting interested in adventure sports.
2 Surfing is a relatively old sport.
3 Ela is not the only older person who enjoys surfing.
4 Marco's friends don't like knitting.
5 Marco thinks knitting is more interesting than yoga.
6 Yarn-bombers paint graffiti on buses.

b Compare your answers with a partner. Correct the ones that are false.

4 Work in pairs. What hobbies are popular with you and your friends and family? Do you know anyone who has an unusual hobby? What do they do?

Act your age!

The media loves stereotypes. How many photos have you seen which show teenagers playing computer games, or grandparents doing the gardening? In real life, of course, we enjoy all kinds of hobbies, at all ages. We've interviewed two people who don't want to 'act their age'.

Ela, 79

I've always liked adventurous sports. Paragliding, skydiving – you name it, I've tried it. On the day I retired, I went surfing. I've never liked taking it easy, 'acting my age'. I haven't lost my love of excitement, just because my hair's gone grey! Surfing has a young image now, but it's an old, old sport – did you know that James Cook first saw people surfing in Tahiti in 1769? For me, it's a great way to stay fit, as well as to meet friends. It can help people in difficult times, too. In 2007, a man called Doc Paskowitz took surfboards to Gaza. He wanted people there to experience happiness and freedom, even in war time. He was 86! Compared to him, I'm still pretty young.

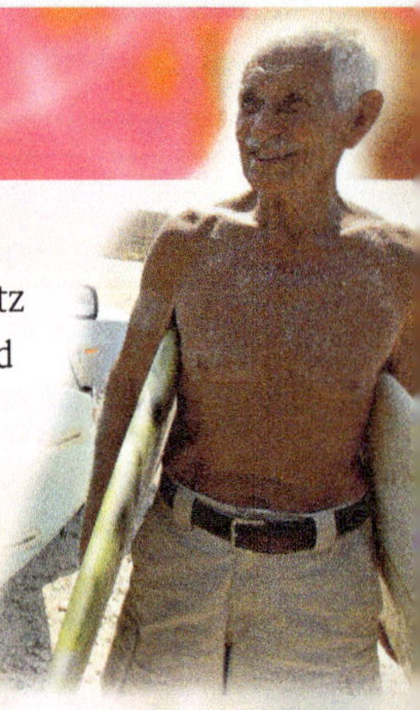

Marco, 15

I'm a knitter. I've knitted hats and scarves, as well as a cover for my iPod. They don't look like things your granny knits! I've used dark colours and added skull and crossbones logos*. They look pretty good! I'm not the only one. In my school in Manhattan, we're allowed to knit in class. Studies have shown that knitting is good

c .... the electric guitar

e .... crafts

Grammar

1 a Complete the sentences using the words in the box. Which part of the article do they come from, Ela's or Marco's?

adventurous sports	a cover for my iPod	excitement	graffiti	knitting	skydiving	taking it easy

1 I**'ve knitted** hats and scarves, as well as ....
2 I**'ve** always **liked** ....
3 **Have** you ever **seen** .... on city streets?
4 Paragliding, ... – you name it, I**'ve tried** it.
5 I**'ve** never **liked** ....
6 I **haven't lost** my love of ....
7 Studies **have shown** that .... is good for stress.

b Look at the verbs in **bold** in the sentences above. Which are describing

1 an action that happened in the past, but we don't know exactly when?
2 a situation or feeling that started in the past and continues in the present?

2 Complete 1–10 in the Grammar Panel.

3 Complete 11 and 12 in the Grammar Panel. Are any of the example sentences true for you? Then complete 13–16.

Present Perfect

Form

To form the present perfect simple we use *have* / *has* + past participle (*done*, *tried*, *seen*).

(+) *I'* (1) .... *tried a lot of different sports.*
(–) *She* (2) .... *lost her love for life.*
(?) (3) .... *you tried knitting?*
(Y/N) *Yes, I* (4) .... *./No, I haven't.*

Past participles

Regular verbs: infinitive + *-ed*
like → (5) ...., *play* → *played*,
knit → (6) ...., *try* → (7) ....

Many verbs have irregular past participles.
do → *done*, *go* → *been*,
see → (8) ...., *show* → (9) ....,
lose → (10) ....

(See Irregular verbs, page 168.)

See page 143 for grammar reference and more practice.

Some common uses

To talk about actions that happened at some time in the past, but we don't say when. (11) ....

To talk about situations or feelings that started in the past and continue to be true in the present.
(12) ....

Time expressions

ever/never
We often use *ever* and *never* to talk about our life experiences.
Have you (13) .... *tried skydiving?*
I've (14) .... *done karate.*

always/never
We often use *always* and *never* to talk about feelings or beliefs we've had for a long time.
I've (15) .... *wanted to try paragliding.*
I've (16) .... *lost my love for playing games.*

*skull and crossbones logo

for stress, so it helps us to learn. I'd definitely rather knit than do yoga! Knitting can be fun, too. In the USA and Canada, there's a craze for 'yarn-bombing'. Have you ever seen graffiti on city streets? Well, it's a bit like that. People cover signs, walls, even buses, in colourful wools. But you can take the knitting off afterwards – not like graffiti!

4 a Write *Have you ever... ?* questions about the hobbies in the photos, and other hobbies. *Have you ever been skateboarding?*

b Ask other students in your class your questions. Make a note of their answers. Which hobby was the most popular?

LISTENING

1 Work in pairs. Look at the webpage and answer the questions.

1 Who are you going to hear?
2 Who is this person going to talk about?
3 What is Missing People?

2 **a** 4.3 Listen to the video. Complete the sentences.

1 Ceri last saw Alun .... months ago.
2 Bethan is Alun's ....
3 Alun disappeared on Friday the .... of ....
4 He was going to meet his friends at the ....
5 Since Alun left, Ceri hasn't been able to ....
6 The Missing People telephone number is ....

b How is Ceri going to spend Christmas? What would she like to happen?

3 Work in groups. Look at the webpage and the photos. Discuss the questions.

- Have you ever seen any notices like these?
- Can you think of any other ideas to help find missing people?
- Do you know any stories about missing people in your country?

home > missing people > campaigns > Message From Mum - Ceri Padarn for Alun

Message From Mum – Ceri Padarn for Alun

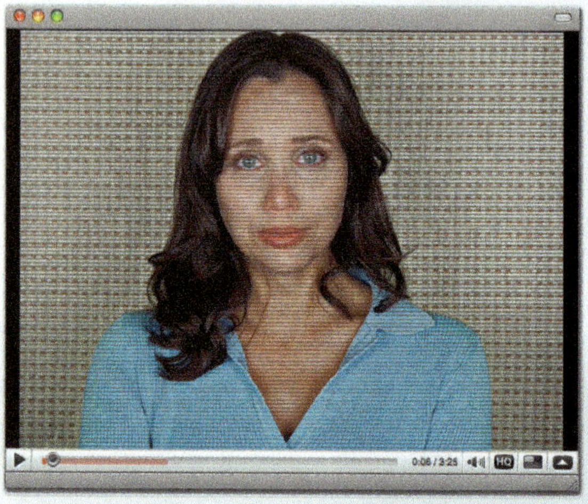

Video appeal for missing Alun Padarn
From: missingpeople

Missing People is the only UK charity that works with missing people, their families and others who care for them.

Please help us find more missing people. Visit our website at www.missingpeople.org.uk. Thank you for your support.

GRAMMAR (1)

1 **a** Underline the verbs in the sentences. Are they present perfect or past simple?

A Have you seen Alun?
B Yes, I've seen him. I saw him last week.

b Choose the correct options for 1–3 in the GRAMMAR PANEL.

2 **a** Write present perfect and past simple questions.

you ever be lost ? what happen ?
Have you ever been lost? *What happened?*

1 you ever stay out all night ?
how you feel ?
2 you ever argue with your parents ?
why you argue ?
3 you ever give money to a charity ?
what the money for ?
4 you ever help a stranger ?
what you do ?
5 you ever say goodbye to someone for a long time ?
what you say ?

b Ask and answer the questions.

PRESENT PERFECT & PAST SIMPLE

We can use both the **present perfect** and the **past simple** to talk about things that happened in the past.

When we use the (1)*past simple / present perfect* we don't say exactly when something happened. This is not important.

I've seen him. NOT ~~*I've seen him last week.*~~
They've found him.

When we use the (2)*past simple / present perfect* we often use a past time expression, e.g. *two days ago, last week.*

I saw him six months ago.
They found him yesterday.

We often use the (3)*past simple / present perfect* to add extra details about a specific past event.

Where did they find him? They found him at the train station.

See page 143 for grammar reference and more practice.

PRONUNCIATION: auxiliary verbs

1 a 4.4 Listen to three short conversations. What have the people lost?

b Listen again and complete the questions.

1 .... you like to wait here while I get it?
2 .... you looking for this?
3 .... you seen my mobile phone?

2 a Listen again and notice the pronunciation of the auxiliary verbs.

1 Would /wəd/ 2 Are /ə/ 3 Have /həv/

b Practise saying the questions in 1b.

LISTENING

1 Work in pairs. Have you ever lost something on public transport? What did you lose? Did you get it back?

2 a 4.5 Listen to a report about the Lost Property office in the centre of Paris. Answer the questions.

1 How long has the office been open?
2 What objects do people lose most frequently?
3 What four strange objects does the reporter mention?

b Listen again. How long has each object been in the lost property office?

1 .... : since last Sunday.
2 .... : for almost a year.
3 .... : since last May.
4 .... : for about five weeks.

3 Discuss in pairs. How do you think these things got lost?

GRAMMAR (2)

1 Look at how the words *for* and *since* are used in LISTENING 2b. Choose the correct option for 1 and 2 in the GRAMMAR PANEL below.

2 Look at the time expressions in the box. Which can you use with

1 for? 2 since?

2010	a long time	I was a child	last night
three years	two weeks		

3 a Think of things you haven't done for each of the time expressions in 2. Write sentences using the present perfect and a time expression.

I haven't seen snow for a long time.

b Work in pairs. Share your sentences with a partner. Do you have anything in common?

4 a Look at the categories below and write the first four answers you think of.

- Two people (other than my family) who are important in my life:
  my best friend, my boyfriend
- Two possessions which are important to me:
  my mobile, my diary

b Work in pairs. Talk about your answers.

- How long have you known/owned them?
- Why are they special to you?

PRESENT PERFECT WITH *FOR* & *SINCE*

When we use the **present perfect** to talk about a situation that started in the past and continues in the present we often use the question *How long... ?* and time expressions with *for* and *since*.

How long have you known her?

We use:

(1)*for / since* to talk about a period of time.

(2)*for / since* to talk about when something started.

I've known her for years.
I've known her since 2009.

See page 143 for grammar reference and more practice.

READING

1 Quickly read the article. Who are Libby, Rosemeri and Ciro? Write summary sentences like the one below. Change the **bold** words.

Libby is a 13-year-old Australian girl who is a teenage carer.

Young achievers

For millions of teenagers, responsibilities begin early.

The carer

A carer looks after an elderly or sick person at home, often a relative. We do not know how many teenage carers there are worldwide, but there are over 180,000 in Australia alone.

Spotlight on:

Libby, 13, Australia

Mum's illness started getting worse a few years ago (she's got multiple sclerosis), and now she needs my help. Dad died when I was young, and I'm the oldest child, so I do most of the housework. I make the breakfast, do jobs around the home, that sort of stuff. I've got four younger sisters, so I'm always busy! The oldest child always does more work, I think.

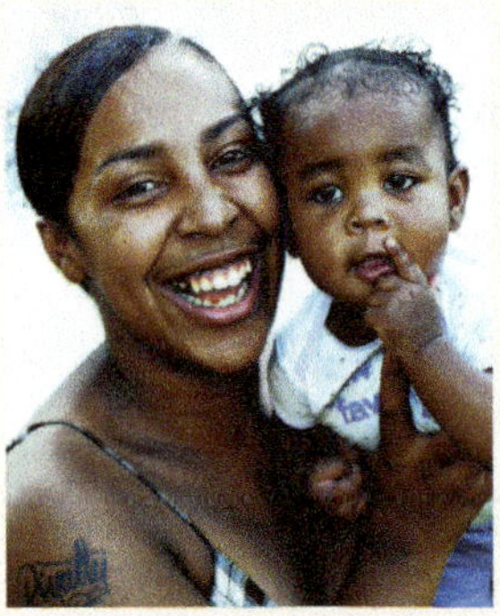

The mum

Every year, more than 13 million teenage girls have a child.

Spotlight on:

Rosemeri, 16, Brazil

Life is certainly easier without kids. Now I've become a mum, I look after Angela, pay the bills, do the shopping and other adult things – I don't have a lot of time for myself. Sometimes I feel jealous of my friends. Going to the beach is much more fun than staying at home with a baby! But I wouldn't change places for anything. Seeing Angela grow up is amazing. It's hard, but becoming a mum is the best thing I've ever done.

The worker

About 158 million under-14-year-olds work. In Latin America, about 16% of children work. The figure is about 22% in Asia and 41% in Africa.

Spotlight on:

Ciro, 12, Bolivia

I've always worked – when I was little, I did the gardening at home and grew vegetables. Now I'm older, I work for much longer hours, sometimes ten or more a day. I work with my father and brothers in the fields. I'm the youngest worker, but I'm faster than my dad! Younger workers are quicker, I think. I left school early. Sometimes I miss it. Having a job is a lot more difficult than studying. But I want to help my family.

NOTICE *ABOUT* **+ NUMBERS**

We can use *about* with numbers, ages and times to mean ***approximately***, ***a little*** or ***more/less than***.

She's about 50. (She may be a little older or younger than 50.)

I'll arrive at about 10 o'clock. (I may arrive a little before or after 10 o'clock.)

2 Read the article again. Choose the correct answer.

1 Which one of the sentences is true about Libby's family?
   a She doesn't have a father.
   b Her mum became ill a few months ago.
   c There are four children in her family.

2 How does Rosemeri feel about being a mum?
   a She does not enjoy it.
   b She thinks it can be hard.
   c She loves everything about it.

3 What does Ciro say about work?
   a He prefers having a job to going to school.
   b He enjoys working with his family.
   c It is more difficult now than it was in the past.

4 Which of the facts is correct?
   a There are more teenage mums than child workers.
   b The biggest number of teenage carers is in Australia.
   c A bigger percentage of children work in Africa than in Asia.

3 Work in small groups. Do you know any 'young achievers' like Libby, Rosemeri or Ciro? What have they done/are they doing?

VOCABULARY: home life

1 Find the expressions in the article and write the missing verbs.

1 .... jobs around the home
2 .... the breakfast
3 .... the shopping
4 .... after children/other people
5 .... the housework
6 .... the bills
7 .... the gardening

2 4.6 Listen to Nico talking about the things he does at home. What does he *often*, *sometimes* and *never* do?

3 **a** Do you help at home? What do you do? How often do you do it? Tell your partner.

b Who helps the most/least?

GRAMMAR

1 Which of the people in the article agrees with the statements? Do you agree?

1 Working is **more difficult** than studying.
2 Life is **easier** without kids.
3 The **oldest** child in a family usually has the **most difficult** time.
4 **Younger** workers are **better** than **older** workers.

2 Complete 1–5 in the GRAMMAR PANEL.

3 **a** Complete the questions about family and home life.

1 Do you have any (**old**) or (**young**) brothers and sisters? How old are they?
2 Who is the (**good**) and the (**bad**) person for doing housework in your family? What do they do?
3 What is the (**busy**) time in your house? Why is it busy?
4 Is your family (**big**) or (**small**) than Libby's? Is it (**easy**) to live in a big or a small family?
5 Who do you think has the (**interesting**) job in your family? What do they do?

b Work in pairs. Ask and answer the questions. Are your families very similar or very different? Share your answers with the class.

4 **a** Add *than* or *the* to the sentences below.

1 My family is one of biggest families in the class.
2 My family is smaller most of the other families in the class.
3 Biggest family is the teacher's family.
4 The person with most interesting job is my partner's father.
5 Most people think it's easier to live in a big family in a small one.
6 Busiest time in most families is breakfast time.

b Change the sentences to make them true for your class.

COMPARATIVES & SUPERLATIVES

We use **comparative adjectives** to compare and contrast two things.

We use **superlative adjectives** to compare and contrast something with all the other items in a group.

	Adjective	Comparative	Superlative
One syllable	old	*older*	(1) ....
Two syllables ending in *-y*	easy	(2)	easiest
Two or more syllables	difficult	(3)	(4) ....
Irregular	good	(5)	best

We often use *than* with comparative adjectives.
*I'm much faster **than** him.*

We usually use *the* or a possessive adjective (*my*, *his*, etc.) before a superlative adjective.
*I'm **the** youngest child. She's **my** best friend.*

See page 143 for grammar reference and more practice.

SPEAKING

1 **a** Make notes comparing your family members. Use the words in the box or your own ideas.

annoying childish lazy friendly
funny intelligent helpful noisy

My sister's the laziest. She's lazier than my brothers!

b Work in groups. Ask and answer questions about your family members.
Who's the laziest person in your family? Why?

2 Tell the rest of the class about the families in your group. Whose family would you most like to live in? Why?

a

b

c

NOTICE *SAY/TELL*

We use an object after *tell*, but we don't use an object after *say*.

He had something to say.
He had something to tell us.

Intonation: sounding enthusiastic

4.8 Listen to the expressions. Pay attention to the way the speakers say the **bold** words.

1 *I've **missed** you.*
2 *It's **great** to see you.*
3 *We **must** meet up again **soon**.*
4 *I've got **lots** to tell you.*

For each of 1–4, decide which speaker sounds the most enthusiastic, a or b.

Practise saying sentences 1–10 in 3a. Be enthusiastic!

TUNE IN

1 Work in pairs. Look at the three photos. Discuss the questions.

- What is the relationship between the people?
- Do you have any family or friends who live a long way away? How do you stay in touch?
- When was the last time you met these friends or relatives? What did you do?

2 4.7 Listen to three conversations and answer the questions.

1 How do the people know each other?
2 How long ago did they last see each other?

FOCUS ON LANGUAGE

3 a Read these extracts from 2. Choose the correct options.

1 Welcome *back / again*!
2 I've *lost / missed* you.
3 So *say / tell* me, how are things?
4 It's great to *see / look* you again.
5 It's been a long time *for / since* we last met.
6 It's good to catch *down / up*.
7 We must meet up again *quickly / soon*.
8 How *are / do* your sons?
9 So, Mum, how's it *doing / going*?
10 I've got lots to *say / tell* you.

b Listen again and check.

4 Work in pairs. Answer the questions.

1 What other questions do people often ask when they're catching up?
2 How do people usually answer these questions?

5 4.9 Listen to the questions from 3a and write the answers.

OVER TO YOU

6 Imagine you are at a class reunion party. You haven't seen the students in your class for five years! Think of five things you would like to ask them.

7 Work in groups.

- Take turns to talk to each person in the group and ask your questions.
- Use the expressions from 3.
- Remember – you're excited to see each other, so sound enthusiastic!

WRITING TASK: AN INFORMAL EMAIL

TUNE IN

1 Read three emails sent through a networking website called *Link Up*. How do the people know María?

Link UP

Search:

Post: Messages • Status • Photos • Videos • Links

María José Carvajal

Hi María!

Great to hear from you! How's it going? I haven't seen you since we left university. That's ages ago! Lots has happened since then. Three years ago I got married to Philippe, and the year after that we moved to France. Have you ever been there? You should visit. I miss you!

Write soon,

Izzie

Reply • Forward • Delete

Dear María,

Do you remember me? We worked at the music shop together a few years ago. Anyway, I've got a new job now, at the tourist centre in town. The music shop was more exciting, but this job pays the bills! What are you up to now? It'd be great to meet up sometime.

All the best,

Xian

Reply • Forward • Delete

Hi there!

Sorry I haven't written sooner. I've been really busy – but in a good way. In January, Mum started her own catering business and she asked me to be her chef. I've never done so much work in all my life!

Love,

Your favourite cousin, Rosa x

PS Do you like my new profile pic?

Reply • Forward • Delete

2 Why do people use websites like *Link Up*? Have you ever used a website like this? Why/Why not?

PREPARE FOR TASK

3 Read the emails again. Find three ways of

1 beginning an email
2 ending an email

4 Work in pairs. Which expressions would you use in an email to a friend?

1 Yours sincerely,
2 Hiya
3 Give me a call sometime!
4 I look forward to hearing from you.
5 Take care,
6 See you soon.
7 I am writing to...
8 Dear Sir / Madam,
9 Best wishes,
10 What's up?

5 Read the emails again and answer the questions.

1 Can you find any more useful informal expressions?
2 Do we use full forms (*I have been*) or short forms (*I've been*) in informal writing?

TASK

6 Think of a friend that you haven't seen for a long time. Make notes about

1 who your friend is.
2 when you last met your friend.
3 what you have done since you last met/ spoke to your friend. Think of at least four things.
4 what you would like to know about your friend now.

7 Imagine you have seen your friend's profile on the *Link Up* website. Write an email to him/her. Use informal expressions.

REPORT BACK

8 Swap your email with another student. Imagine you wrote to each other. Write a short reply (50–100 words).

➜ Go to Review B, Unit 4, p. 68

5 LIVE AND LEARN

a

b

c

1 Work in pairs. Look at the photos of different learning situations and discuss the questions.

- Who is the teacher?
- Who are the students?
- Where are they?
- What are they studying?

2 a 5.1 Listen and answer the questions.
1 Who's speaking, the teachers or the students?
2 What's special about each teaching situation?

b Listen again. Complete the statements with Professor Quarashi (PQ), Matthew Sanford (MS) or Phil Higgins (PH).
1 .... thinks classrooms are ugly places.
2 .... believes everyone can do something special.
3 .... teaches IT.
4 .... teaches at secondary school.
5 .... teaches at a university.
6 .... teaches Science.
7 .... flies to class.
8 .... teaches in the USA.

3 a Work in pairs. Think about a teacher who made an impression on you. What was special about him/her? Tell your partner.

b Share your experiences with the class. Do you think any of the teachers could be 'Teacher of the Year'?

4 a Look at A in the KEY VOCABULARY PANEL. Put the subjects in the correct category. Can you add any more subjects?

b Look again at the list in A and answer the questions.
- Which of these subjects have you studied? Are you studying any now?
- Are there any you would like to study in the future? Why?

5 a Look at B in the KEY VOCABULARY PANEL. Do these types of school exist in your country? Use a dictionary to help you. What is the age group for each one?

b Match the qualifications to the types of school.

6 Work in pairs. Tell your partner about the schools you have attended and the qualifications you have.

7 a 5.2 Listen to Keira talking about a course she is doing. What makes her course different from the ones in the photos? Is she enjoying it? Why/Why not?

b Work in groups. Have you ever done a course online? If yes, what did you think of the experience? If not, would you like to? Why/Why not?

KEY VOCABULARY

Education & learning

A Academic subjects

Art Biology Business Studies
Chemistry Drama Economics
Geography History
IT (Information Technology)
Languages Literature Mathematics
Music Philosophy Physics
Politics Psychology Sport

Arts: ....
Sciences: ....
Social Sciences: ....
Other: ....

B Schools & qualifications

SCHOOLS

high school kindergarten
pre-school primary school
secondary school technical college
university

QUALIFICATIONS

degree masters
professional diploma
school leaving certificate
vocational qualification

NOTICE *CAREER, COURSE, STUDIES*

Use *career* to talk about someone's professional life.
Use *course* or *studies* to talk about education.

During his long career as a teacher, he lived in the USA.
I've just finished a course at university.
As part of his university studies, he travelled to India.

How do you say *career*, *course* and *studies* in your language?

- PRACTISE FUTURE PLANS
- TALK ABOUT COURSES & STUDYING

SPEAKING & READING

1 Work in pairs. Look at the photos. What does each photo show?

2 **a** Match photos a–d to the university courses.

1 Sports Science 2 Equine Studies 3 Social Networking Studies 4 Forensic Science

b Discuss the questions with your partner.

- What's the link between these courses and the title of the article?
- What are 'traditional' subjects?
- Would you like to study any of the subjects in the photos? What do you think the course would include?
- Can you think of any other 'non-traditional' subjects which are popular in your country?

3 Look at the expressions highlighted in red in the article. Can you guess what they mean?

Degrees with a difference

In many countries, students can choose between hundreds or thousands of degree courses. With these choices, it's hard for students to **make up their minds** and choose just one! Many 'traditional' subjects, like Physics, Geography and Languages, are now much less popular. So which trendier subjects are **taking their place**?

The number of students taking these courses has rapidly grown in the past decade:

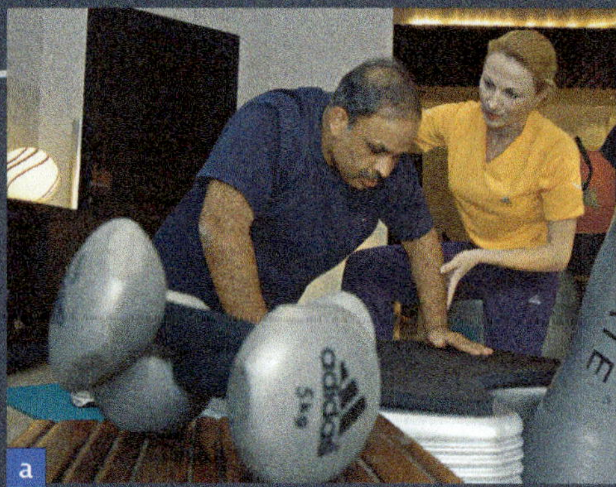
a

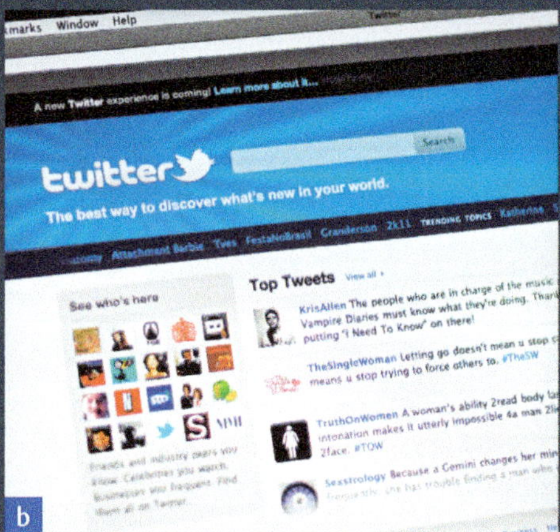

b

c

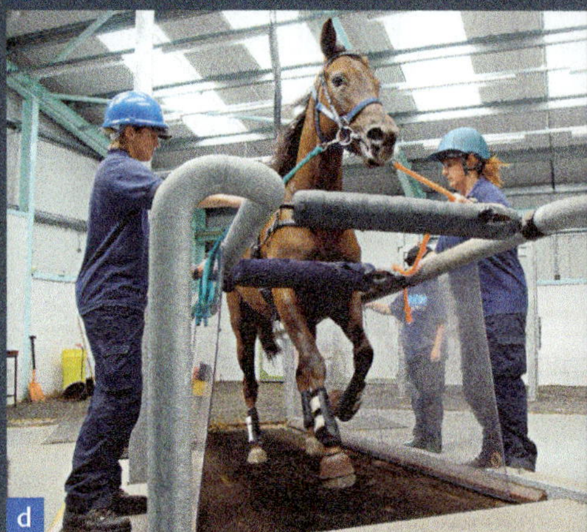
d

LISTENING

1 **a** 5.3 Listen to three people talking about their university studies. Match the people to three of the photos.

b Listen again. Choose the correct answer, a or b, for each speaker.

1 Ilaria chose her course because
  a it will be easy to get a job with this degree.
  b the subject looked interesting in TV shows.
2 Raushan's very interested in learning more about
  a health.
  b psychology.
3 Lee chose his subject because
  a he already knows a lot about it.
  b his parents think it's a good idea.

2 **a** Complete the statements with the correct name, Ilaria, Raushan or Lee.

1 .... lives in a country where horses are important.
2 .... likes police dramas.
3 ....'s parents don't approve of his/her choice.

b Read transcript 5.3 on page 164 and check your answers.

3 Do you think some degree subjects are more useful than others? Which ones? Why?

Grammar

1 **a** Look at the sentences. Who is speaking, Ilaria or Lee?

1 **I'm taking** my final exam next month.
2 **I'm working** really hard for this exam.
3 **I'm starting** the course next year.
4 **I'm getting** excited about it already.

b Which sentences refer to a) the future? b) the present? Underline the future time expressions. Then complete 1 and 2 in the Grammar panel.

2 **a** Write the verbs in brackets in the present continuous. Use the affirmative or negative to make the sentences true for you. Which sentences refer to the future?

1 I .... *(work)* really hard at the moment.
2 I .... *(go)* shopping after class.
3 I .... *(stay)* in tomorrow night.
4 I .... *(cook)* dinner for friends at the weekend.

b Compare your sentences with a partner. Then write two more about

a things you're doing at the moment.
b plans you have for the near future.

3 **a** Read transcript 5.3 on page 164. What other verb form is used to describe future plans?

b Complete 3 in the Grammar panel.

4 **a** Look at the questions. Which can you rewrite using *going to*?

1 Are you studying for an exam at the moment?
2 What are you doing next weekend?
3 How are you getting home tonight?
4 Are you reading a book at the moment? If yes, are you enjoying it?

b Ask and answer the questions in pairs.

Speaking

1 Work in small groups. You are going to design a new university course. Follow the instructions.

1 Think of a subject that isn't offered at universities in your country.
2 Decide why it might be useful or interesting. (Is it going to help students get a job? Is it related to youth culture? Is it related to new technologies?)
3 Decide what kind of information and skills the course is going to cover and how long it's going to last.

2 Present your course to the class. Which course is

a the most unusual? Why?
b the most useful? Why?

Present continuous & *going to*

Present continuous

We use the **present continuous** to talk about

1 the present (what we are doing now or around now):
I'm working really hard for this exam.
(1) ....

2 plans and arrangements for the future (with a fixed time or date).
I'm starting the course next year.
(2) ....

Going to

We also use ***going to*** to talk about future plans and intentions.

There is very little difference between the present continuous and *going to* for future plans and arrangements.
What are you studying next year? OR *What are you going to study next year?*
I'm starting a degree in September. OR
(3) ....

We often use the **present continuous** for fixed (diary) arrangements & ***going to*** for more general plans or intentions:
I'm starting French classes next Tuesday.
I'm going to study French one day.

See page 144 for grammar reference and more practice.

Notice *gonna*

In very informal writing, e.g. in emails to friends, text messages and online chats, we often write ***gonna*** instead of ***going to***.
Gonna study after class today. Speak tomorrow!
We're gonna miss you! Have a good trip.

It's also common to see *gonna* in song lyrics and advertising slogans.
Never gonna give you up...
It's gonna be big!

VOCABULARY: *-ed/-ing* adjectives

1 a Work in pairs. Choose the options which best describe your experience of school.

1 I usually felt *bored* / *interested* in class.
2 Maths lessons were *confusing* / *exciting*.
3 Homework was usually *boring* / *interesting*.
4 I was always *depressed* / *excited* on Sundays. School started on Monday morning!

b 5.4 Listen. Underline the best option. How do the speakers feel? Who likes/doesn't like school?

2 Look at the pairs of adjectives in 1. Which ones describe

1 how somebody feels?
I am...
2 something that makes a person feel a certain way?
My lessons are...

3 Write sentences with the correct adjectives.

annoyed / annoying fascinated / fascinating
pleased / pleasing tired / tiring

1 This subject ....

2 These students ....

3 I've passed! I / really ....

4 Stop it! You / really ....

4 a Think about your English lessons. Make the questions.

1 What was the most *interesting* / *interested* thing you learnt last week?
2 Which lessons are the most *tired* / *tiring*: morning lessons or afternoon lessons?
3 What do you do when you are *confused* / *confusing* in class?

b Ask and answer the questions.

PRACTISE *MUST* & *MUSTN'T* FOR OBLIGATION
TALK ABOUT RULES

READING

1 Look at the photos and answer the questions.

1 What country do you think they show?
2 What is the boy doing in each one?
3 Where do you think he is in the first one?

2 Read the article quickly and check your ideas. Who is Anselmo? What do the photos tell us about his life?

3 Read the article again. Find and correct the false sentences.

1 Ester thinks Anselmo is an annoying student.
2 Students with low marks can't go to the school.
3 Ester thinks that the most important thing students learn is that life can be difficult.
4 Students don't pay any money to the school.
5 Anselmo didn't enjoy his job.
6 Anselmo wants to work in the circus.

4 Would you like to go to this school? Why/Why not?

THE SCHOOL OF FUN

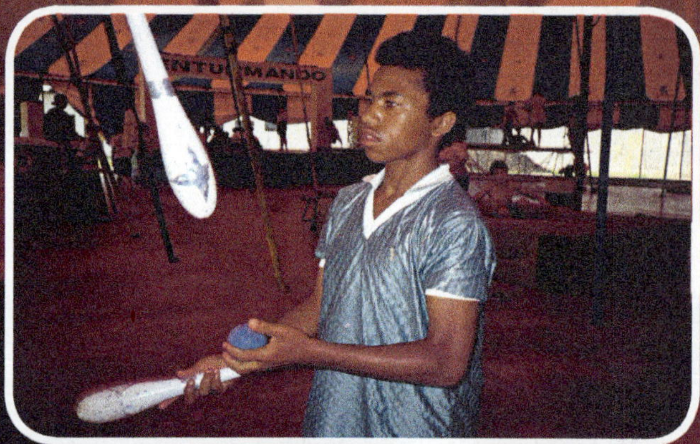

At school yesterday, Anselmo rode a bicyle in the classroom. Then he stood on his head. But his teacher wasn't angry. 'Excellent, Anselmo! I'm really pleased!' Ester da Silva said.

Anselmo goes to an unusual school in Rio de Janeiro, in Brazil. At the school, students aged 4 to 24 learn how to dance, sing and do acrobatics in a circus.

That sounds exciting, but it isn't easy. 'Students have to work hard,' says Ester. 'We say that all students at Circus School have to study 'normal' school subjects like Languages and Maths as well – that's very important. They don't have to get the highest marks, but they do

Grammar

1 a Read the sentences. Are they true for Anselmo's school?

1 All the students **have to** work hard.
2 They **don't have to** study Languages and Maths.
3 They **mustn't** be late for class.
4 They **must** always be polite to their teachers.

b Check your answers in the article in Reading 1.

2 a Look at the sentences in 1a again. Which talk about

a rules the students always need to follow?
b things it isn't necessary for the students to do?

b Look at the verbs in **bold** in 1a. Use them to complete 1–4 in the Grammar panel.

have to try their best. They mustn't be late for classes, and they must always be polite.'

Ester thinks that Circus School teaches students many useful things. 'Students learn how to work with other people, and they learn about themselves, too. They see that some things in life can be difficult, but if you work hard they can get better. Best of all, they learn that school – and life – can be exciting and enjoyable!'

Circus School is a charity, and all the classes are free. Most of the students come from *favelas* (poor parts of town), where many children leave school without any qualifications. Anselmo lives in a tiny room with his mother and three brothers. He left secondary school when he was 12, and he washed cars for money. 'It was tiring, and many drivers didn't pay.' Now, thanks to Ester, he's hoping for a better future. 'I'm probably not going to be a circus star!' he says, smiling. 'But I might be a teacher one day, like Mrs da Silva. I'm very happy I don't have to clean cars any more!'

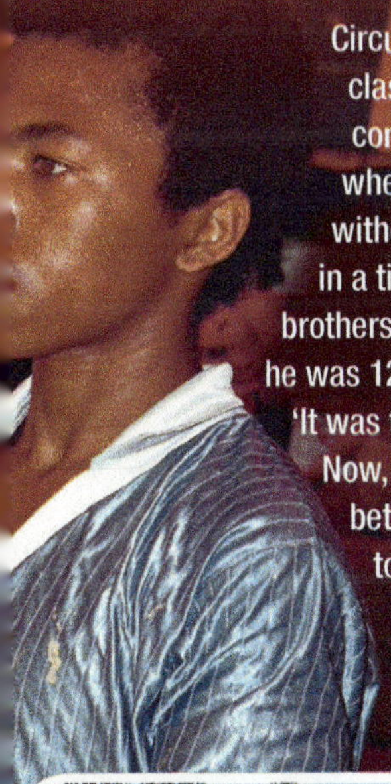

3 a Read the information and choose the correct option. Sometimes both options are correct.

In Japanese schools, there are many rules. They are called *Kosaku*. Here are some examples:

- Students [1] *must / have to* wear a uniform. They can't even choose their own socks!
- Boys [2] *mustn't / don't have to* grow their hair longer than their ears. They can only have short hair. Girls [3] *mustn't / don't have to* have short hair. They can have it long or short.
- Students [4] *must / mustn't* be on time. Late students can't go into class.
- Students [5] *must / mustn't* have jobs. Teachers think that students who work are too tired to study.
- Students [6] *mustn't / don't have to* stay in every night, but if they want to go out, they [7] *must / have to* ask their teacher – even at the weekend!

b Are any of these rules true for schools in your country? Write three more sentences about schools in your country using *have to*, *must*, *mustn't* or *don't have to*.

Must(n't) & (don't) have to for obligation

Must & have/has to

We use *must* and [1] .... to talk about rules and obligations.

Have to is more common than [2] ....

*We **must/have to** be at school at 8 a.m.*
*Anselmo **must/has to** work hard at school.*

Mustn't & don't/doesn't have to

We use [3] .... to talk about prohibition – about things that are against the rules.

We use [4] .... to explain that there is no obligation or rule.

You mustn't be late for school. (= this is one of the rules, you don't have a choice)

*Anselmo **doesn't have to** wash cars anymore.* (= it isn't necessary for him to wash cars now)

See page 144 for grammar reference and more practice.

Speaking

1 Work in groups. Imagine you are going to write the rules for your English class next week. Discuss your ideas.

Students don't have to do any exams. Great idea!

2 Make a poster with your five best ideas.

- Practise adjectives & prepositions
- Talk about museums & culture

Speaking & Reading

1 Work in pairs. Look at this photo. Discuss the questions.

- Do you enjoy visiting museums?
- When was the last time you went to a museum? What did you learn?
- Have you ever used an 'audio guide'? Do you think they're a good idea?

2 **a** Read part of a museum brochure. Where is the museum and what can visitors learn about?

b Have you got any museums like this in your town?

The Museum of Romany Culture isn't a big museum, but it's a fascinating one. At the museum, you can learn about the history of the Romany people in the Czech Republic and around the world. You can also learn about Romany culture and art – and buy some amazing souvenirs in the shop!

You can find the museum in Brno, in the centre of the city's Romany district.

Listening

1 5.5 Listen to the audio guide. In what order do you learn about

- language?
- crafts?
- music?

2 Listen again. Complete the summaries in the museum brochure.

Notice *learn/teach*

I'm learning Romany. (I'm a student.)
I'm teaching Romany. (I'm a teacher.)
She teaches us Romany.
NOT *She ~~learns us~~ Romany.*

A Romany musicians prefer to play instruments like the accordian or the (1) ...., rather than the (2) .... Romany music has inspired musicians like the (3) .... player Django Reinhardt (Belgium) and the punk band Gogol Bordello ((4) ....).

B Today, most Romany people live in (5) .... or (6) ...., but not in wagons. Traditional Romany crafts and clothes are often (7) .... because this is a lucky colour. At the museum, (8) .... can learn these crafts.

C A lot of Roma people speak Romany, but they don't (9) .... or (10) .... the language. In the past, many Romany people told stories about their (11) .... and tradition. At the museum, we teach visitors these stories. You can also buy (12) .... in the gift shop!

3 Work in pairs. Discuss the questions.

- In your region, what are the traditional:
  a) foods? *(pasta, wine...)* b) hobbies or activities? *(music, story-telling...)*
- What traditional things can you do or make?

PRONUNCIATION: stress in two-syllable words

1 5.6 Work in pairs. Complete the table with words from the audio guide. Listen and check.

children enjoy goodbye guitar language lucky ~~music~~ people prefer stories

•●	●•
	music

2 a Is the word stress more often on the first or the second syllable?

b Can you think of two more words for each category?

VOCABULARY: adjectives + prepositions

1 Read the museum's activity programme. How many activities are there?

Museum Activity Programme

All activities are free, and everyone is welcome!

Lectures

Romany culture – 1900 to present day

Workshops

Written and spoken Romany – beginners
Music – all levels
Romany dancing – all levels
Romany crafts – make your own basket!

Other events

Film night

2 5.7 Listen to six museum visitors. Choose the best activity for each visitor.

3 a Match 1–7 to a–g.

1 I'm **bad**
2 I'm quite **good**
3 I'm really **interested**
4 Flamenco is quite **similar**
5 I always get **excited**
6 Japanese is quite **different**
7 I'm **bored**

a **from** Romany.
b **about** the cinema.
c **with** reading.
d **in** history.
e **at** art.
f **at** music.
g **to** some Romany dances.

b Listen again and check.

4 a Complete the sentences about you. Use the correct preposition after each adjective.

I'm completely different from my sister.

1 I'm really good ....
2 One person who's quite similar .... me is ....
3 I sometimes get quite bored ....
4 My best friend and I are both interested ....
5 I always get excited ....
6 When I was young, I was bad ....

b Compare your answers with your partner. Give extra details.

I'm completely different from my sister. She works hard at school. I don't!

5 a Imagine you are visiting the museum. You only have time to go to one event. Which one would you choose?

b Find another student who would like to go with you.

Would you like to go to the... ?
Yes, I'd love to. I'm (really) interested in... / (quite) good at...
Sorry, I'm not interested in / not very good at...

NOTICE REQUESTS WITH *CAN, COULD & WOULD*

We often use the modal forms *can*, *could* and *would* in polite questions and requests.

Can/Could I have some more, please?
I'd like some more, please.

Could and *would* are more formal than *can*.

Intonation: sounding polite

5.9 Listen and write three requests. You will hear each request twice.

Listen again. For each request, decide which speaker sounds more polite, a or b.

Do the polite requests have rising (↗) or falling (↘) intonation?

Work in pairs. Practise the polite conversations in the transcript on page 164.

TUNE IN

1 Look at the photo. What do you notice about it? Do you have a café at your school, university or workplace? Is it similar or different to this?

2 5.8 Listen to five conversations. Which students were polite?

3 Work in groups. Discuss the questions.

- Do you think most people are polite?
- Can you think of any times when you heard someone being impolite? What happened?

FOCUS ON LANGUAGE

4 Are these expressions from the conversations polite (P) or impolite (I)?

1 I want a hamburger.
2 I'd like some curry, please.
3 Give me that, too.
4 What would you like?
5 Can I have the lasagne, please?
6 Please could I have some curry?
7 What can I get you?
8 I'll have some chips.

5 **a** Look at five ways people answered requests. Which reply is NOT polite?

1 Of course.
2 I'm sorry, but...
3 Certainly.
4 I'm afraid...
5 Whatever.

b Complete the table with the polite replies.

Positive (+)	..................., ...
Negative (–)	..................., ...

OVER TO YOU

6 Work in pairs. Choose two of the photos. What are the people doing?

7 For each photo, think of a question or request someone might ask in this situation.

8 Write a short conversation for each photo. Use polite questions and replies.

9 Work in pairs. Practise your conversations.

TUNE IN

1 Look at the extracts from advertisements for three different language schools. Which countries are they in? Discuss which course you'd like the most and why.

a

b

c

PREPARE FOR TASK

2 5.10 Listen to a student asking about one of the courses and answer the questions.

1 Which course is he asking about?
2 Do you think he will go on the course? Why/Why not?

3 **a** Listen again and complete the first column in the table.

Name of school: Adventures in English		Question
1 Accommodation?		
2 Courses – which subjects?		
3 Class size?		
4 Activities?		
5 Price?		

b What questions did the student ask? Complete the second column with the questions. Check your answers in the transcript on page 164.

TASK

4 Work in pairs. Student A, turn to page 159. Student B, turn to page 160. Have your conversations. Remember to be polite.

REPORT BACK

5 Now that you have more information about the schools, which course would you choose? Is there a favourite course in the class?

→ Go to Review B, Unit 5, p. 69 → Go to Writing bank 3, p. 154

6 HELP!

a

b

d

e

1 **a** Work in pairs. What's the connection between the photos and the title of the unit? What do you think is the problem in each photo?

b Look at A in the KEY VOCABULARY PANEL. Which words in the box can you see in the photos? Which words don't match with any of the photos? Which refer to people and which to services? Use a dictionary to help you.

2 **a** 6.1 Listen to three people talking about three of the situations in the photos. Match the situation to the photo.

b Listen again and answer the questions.

- Who's teaching someone? What are they teaching?
- Who phoned the firefighters? Why?
- What did the boy do? Why?

3 Work in groups. Discuss the questions.

- Which person in the photos do you think was most grateful for the help? Why?
- Do you know anyone who does voluntary work for a charity or works for the emergency services? What do they do?
- When was the last time you helped someone with a problem? What was the problem? How did you help them?

4 Look at B in the KEY VOCABULARY PANEL. Complete the table. Use a dictionary to help you.

c

f

5 **a** Complete the sentences with adjectives from B. Sometimes there is more than one adjective.

1 I'm .... when it comes to repairing cars. I really don't know anything about engines.
2 I can be very .... sometimes. I'm always dropping or breaking things!
3 I'm very .... to my parents and my family for all they've done for me.
4 I feel really sorry for .... people. It must be very scary not having a roof over your head.
5 The list of things I have to do today is .... ! I don't think I'll be able to do them all!
6 I find exercises like this very ....

b Work in pairs. Are any of the sentences true for you? Share your answers with your partner.

KEY VOCABULARY

Help

A Jobs & services

ambulance driver breakdown service charity worker doctor emergency services firefighter helpline passer-by police officer rescue worker volunteer

- Can you think of any more people or services to add to the list?

B Adjective suffixes *-ful* & *-less*

Root word	-ful	-less
care	(1)	careless
end		endless
gratitude	grateful	
help	(2)	helpless
home		(3) ....
hope	(4)	hopeless
use	(5)	(6) ....

Note

-ful means that there's a lot of the quality.
hopeful – with a lot of hope
-less means that there's nothing of that quality.
homeless – without a home
Not all root words can take both suffixes.

Notice *the & a/an + adjective*

We can use *the* + adjective to talk about a group of people in general terms.
the young, the elderly, the homeless
But you cannot use *a/an* + adjective.
~~*a young, an elderly, a homeless*~~
With *a/an* + adjective you need a noun.
a young woman, an elderly man, a homeless person

- PRACTISE MODAL VERBS: *CAN/CAN'T* & *SHOULD/SHOULDN'T*
- DISCUSS PEOPLE CHANGING THEIR LIVES

READING

1 **a** Work in groups. Look at the photos and read the headline. What do you think the article is about?

1. People playing football in a competition to make money to give to homeless people.
2. Homeless people from all over the world watching a football tournament.
3. Homeless people playing football in a tournament.

b Read the article. Were you right?

THE HOMELESS WORLD CUP

Most people think that we **should** try to get homeless people off the streets and back to work. But few people have good ideas about how they **can** help.

Mel Young from Scotland and Harald Schmied from Austria had a great idea. They are the founders of the Homeless World Cup (HWC). The HWC is an international football tournament for people who are homeless. The event is held every year and began in 2003 in Austria. At first, people said things like 'homeless people **can't** play football' or 'they **shouldn't** waste time and money organising football matches, they **should** help the homeless find work'. But Young and Schmied saw football as a way to change people's lives and to help them feel good about themselves and get out of poverty. Thirty-one of the original 141 players from the 2003 tournament had a job one year after the tournament.

The impact is getting stronger each year and today about 73% of players make a positive change in their lives after taking part in the HWC. After playing in the HWC, players come off drugs and alcohol. They move into jobs. They get training and education. They get in contact with their families again and they get somewhere to live. Some have even become professional or semi-professional football players or coaches.

So perhaps we **should** all think again about how to help the homeless instead of thinking that we **can't** do anything. We **can** make a difference. It seems that finding a passion such as playing sport **can** help homeless people to find their way in life again.

2 Read the article again. Mark the statements true (T) or false (F). Correct the false ones.

1. Mel Young and Harald Schmied are from the same place.
2. The first HWC was in Austria.
3. There were fewer than 150 players in the first HWC.
4. Players from the HWC usually stay homeless.
5. All players in the HWC become professional football players.

3 Work in groups. Discuss the questions.

- Do you think the writer is in favour of or against the Homeless World Cup? How do you know?
- Do you think the Homeless World Cup is a good idea? Why/Why not?

GRAMMAR

1 **a** Look at the article in READING 1 again. Underline phrases which mean:

1. It's a good idea to help homeless people get off the streets.
2. Homeless people don't know how to play football.
3. It isn't a good idea to waste time and money organising football matches.
4. It's possible to make a difference.

b Look at the verbs in **bold** in your answers to 1a. Complete 1–4 in the GRAMMAR PANEL with the correct sentence.

NOTICE *THE THING IS*

The thing is... is a useful phrase to introduce the main point or problem that we want to talk about.

The thing is, I would like a higher salary.

2 6.2 Listen to the conversation and answer the questions.

1 How do the speakers know each other?
2 Why does Jason want time off?
3 Does Natalie say yes or no?

3 **a** Listen again. Match 1–5 to a–e.

1 Can I take	a ask for time off on the same day.
2 You should	b say no, can I?
3 I can	c finish the report this evening.
4 I can't	d finish that report for the presentation tomorrow.
5 You shouldn't	e this afternoon off as holiday?

b Check your answers in transcript 6.2 on page 165. Find more examples of *can('t)* and *should(n't)*.

4 **a** Work in pairs. Do you agree with Jason or Natalie? Why/Why not?

b What else should/shouldn't you do at work? Share your ideas with the class. Which ones do you agree/disagree with?

You shouldn't surf the internet.

Modal verbs: *can/can't*, *should/shouldn't*

Can/Can't

We use ***can*** or ***can't*** to talk about

1 ability

(+) *I can speak three languages.*

(–) (1) ....

2 possibility

(+) (2) ....

(–) *I'm sorry, I can't come to the meeting today.*

Should/Shouldn't

We use ***should*** to say you think something is a good idea, or the right thing to do.

(3) ....

We use ***shouldn't*** to say you think something is a bad idea, or the wrong thing to do.

(4) ....

Both *can* and *should* are modal verbs. We use them

1 with the infinitive without ~~to~~
2 to make negative sentences and questions:

I can't swim. Can you?
I shouldn't eat any more. Should we order coffee?

See page 145 for grammar reference and more practice.

Listening & Speaking

1 **a** 6.3 Work in pairs. Listen to the people discussing a film and complete the advert.

The PURSUIT *of* HAPPYNESS

Starring Will Smith and Jaden Smith

The true story of Chris Gardner, who loses everything and becomes (1) ....

He has to sleep in a shelter with his young (2) .... He finally gets a (3) ...., but he has to do (4) .... months of training first.

See this on (5) .... at 9 p.m.

b Why should you see the film according to Sameera? More than one answer is correct.

1 The story's good.
2 It's romantic.
3 It's quite sad.
4 It has a happy ending.

2 Would you like to see the film or read the book? Why/Why not? If you have already seen it, what did you think?

3 Think about another film or story that you know and give two reasons why someone should see it or read about it.

You should see it because...

- PRACTISE PREDICTIONS WITH *WILL, MAY, MIGHT*
- TALK ABOUT LIFE COACHES

a

b

d

e

c

VOCABULARY: senses

1 Work in pairs. Look at photos a–e. Match the sense verbs and adjectives to make sentences.

feel look smell sound taste

delicious loud soft stunning terrible

Oysters taste delicious when they're fresh!

2 **a** Make more phrases with the ten words in 1a. What can you describe?

Freshly baked bread smells delicious!

b Add other adjectives to the verbs to make five more sentences. Use a dictionary to help you.

His voice sounds very quiet...

3 Work in pairs. Use the verbs in 1a to describe

1 your favourite dinner.
2 someone you met recently.
3 a pet/animal you like.
4 your favourite music.
5 a place you've visited.

4 Work in pairs. Student A, turn to page 159. Student B, turn to page 160. Take turns to describe and guess what the image shows.

"Intonation: positive or negative"

6.4 Listen to six expressions. Is the speaker saying something positive or negative?

6.5 Listen again. Write what they say.

Work in pairs. Practise saying the expressions. Your partner says if you sound positive or negative.

LISTENING

1 Work in pairs. Look at the pictures. What problem do you think each person has?

a

b

c

d

2 6.6 Listen and check your ideas. Match the speakers' problems 1–4 to pictures a–d.

3 **a** Match advice i–iv to problems 1–4.

i leave him / talk to him
ii stay at home / leave home
iii get more training / change jobs
iv talk to her / don't tell her

b 6.7 Listen and choose the correct advice for each problem.

4 Work in pairs. Discuss the questions.

- Which is the most serious problem?
- Do you agree with the advice?
- What do you think the people should do?

GRAMMAR

1 **a** Work in pairs. Read the predictions using *will*, *may* and *might*. Match 1–7 to a–g.

1 He may not
2 They might be
3 They'll tell me
4 She'll give you
5 You may need to
6 She might not be
7 She may have

a a problem with her sense of smell.
b if they want you to leave.
c angry, because she's your friend.
d have another girlfriend.
e some ideas.
f happy that you still live there.
g talk to your boss.

b 6.7 Listen again and check.

2 **a** Answer the questions.

1 Which sentences show the speaker is sure about the prediction?
2 Which show the speaker is talking about a possibility?
3 What is the negative form of *may* and *might*?

b Complete 1–4 in the GRAMMAR PANEL.

3 **a** Write predictions about your future with the prompts and *will/won't* and *may/might (not)*.

1 travel / all over the world
2 pass / my exams
3 get / my dream job
4 make / lots more friends
5 be / rich or famous

b Write two more predictions about yourself.

PREDICTIONS: *WILL, MAY, MIGHT*

USE

We use ***will***, ***may*** or ***might*** + infinitive (without *to*) to make predictions about the future.

We use (1) .... when we are sure.

We use (2) .... or (3) .... when we are not completely sure.

FORM

\+ subject + *will/might/may* + verb: *I might lose my job.*

– subject + (4) .... */might not/may not* + verb: *He may not come tonight.*

NOTE:

We never say or write *may not* as a contraction. We sometimes say *mightn't* but it isn't very common.

We also use *I think* or *I don't think* in predictions with *will*.

I don't think he will do well, NOT ~~*I think he won't*~~ *do well.*

See page 145 for grammar reference and more practice.

Have you got what it takes to be a life coach?

If you are a friendly, active person who wants to help people, life coaching might be the right career for you.

a Life coaches are trained professionals who help their clients with a problem in their life. They will help people improve their lives in specific ways.

b They may meet with their clients in person, on the telephone or even online and by email. Life coaches work with clients in many ways and help them to have less stress, use their time better and set goals for the future.

c You should first decide what kind of life coach you want to be. You may want to work in finance or relationships. Or you might want to work in careers or how people spend their time. Then you should talk to a person who is already a life coach and discuss your ideas. Then you can sign up for a course at a college and start your new career!

READING

1 Look at the illustration and read the introduction to the web article. Do you know anything about this type of career? What do you think it involves?

2 Read the article. Match questions 1–3 to paragraphs a–c.

1 What does a life coach do?
2 How can I become a life coach?
3 What is a life coach?

3 Read the questions in 2 again. Answer each question in your own words.

SPEAKING

1 **a** Work in groups. Think about a time when you gave someone advice. Discuss the questions.

- Who was the person? *(friend, family member, co-worker, partner)*
- What kind of advice was it? *(relationship, finance, study, job)*
- What did you say? *(You should..., You shouldn't..., This will/might happen.)*
- Do you think you helped the other person?

b Compare your answers with other groups.

6.3 WHERE DOES IT HURT?

- Practise vocabulary to describe ailments
- Discuss good health & Chinese medicine

VOCABULARY: health problems

1 Work in pairs. Look at the photos. What is wrong with the people? Match the statements to the photos.

1 I have a terrible headache. I can't go to work today.

2 I fell off my motorbike and broke my leg.

3 My ear hurts. I think I have an ear infection.

4 My daughter has a sore throat. We're going to the doctor this afternoon.

2 What should you do when you have the problems in 1? Choose from the list.

- see a doctor
- have an X-ray
- stay in bed
- see a dentist
- take a painkiller
- rest
- drink liquids

NOTICE *HURT/ACHE*

Hurt and *ache* are verbs (*my stomach aches/hurts*), but *ache* is also a noun (*I have a stomachache*. NOT *I have a stomach ~~hurt~~*).

PRONUNCIATION: word stress

1 a 6.8 Listen and complete the words and phrases.

backache, a (1) .... , toothache,
an (2) .... infection,
indigestion, my (3) .... hurts,
my (4) .... hurts,
a sore (5) ....

b Listen again and underline the word stress.

2 Listen and repeat with the correct word stress.

LISTENING & SPEAKING

1 a 6.9 Work in pairs. Listen to the conversations. Where are the people?

b Listen again and complete the table.

What is wrong	What to do
(1)	....
(2)	....
(3)	....
(4)	....

2 Look at the photos. What health problems might the people have? Describe what is wrong with the people and what they should do.

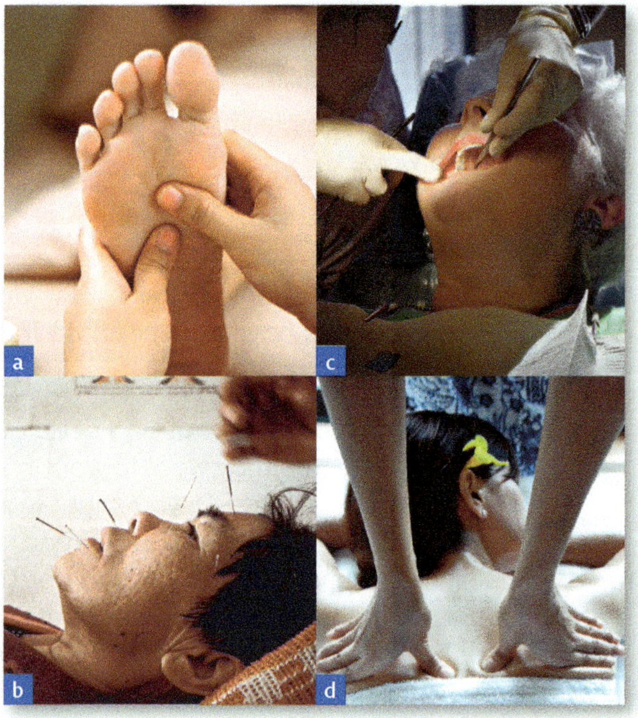

3 Work in groups. Describe the problems. Who has the worst problem? Who gives the best advice?

Reading

1 Read the first part of the information leaflet. Label the four parts of the face in **bold**.

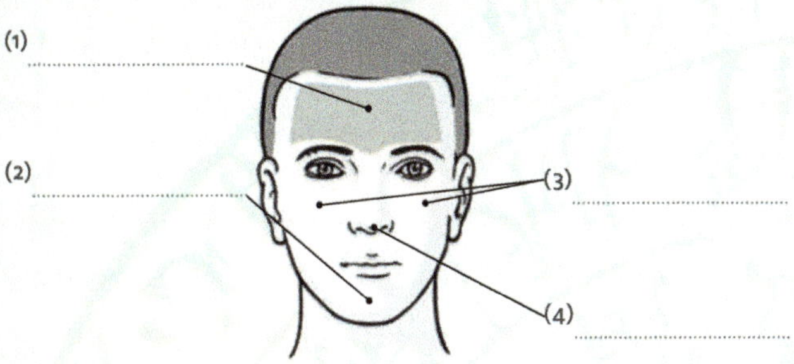

What do you see when you look in the mirror? According to Chinese medicine, your face can give you information about your health. Your **forehead**, **nose**, **chin** and **cheeks** can tell you what is happening inside your body.

2 Read the second part of the information leaflet. Complete the chart.

Problem on face	What it might mean
1 red forehead	• heart problem or .... problem
2 a spot on your nose	• ....
3 red nose	• ....
4 dark skin around chin or mouth	• problems with the .... or ....
5 skin problem on right cheek	• illness in the ....
6 red right cheek	• getting a ....
7 red left cheek	• a .... problem
8 problems with cheeks	• .... illness

Read on to find out what your face says about you.

FOREHEAD According to Chinese medicine, the forehead is connected to the heart, as well as the mind and spirit. If your forehead looks red, it may show that you have a heart problem or it might be because you have recently had a difficult relationship problem.

NOSE Your nose has a connection to the stomach. If you have a spot on your nose, your choice of food may be the problem. As a result, you may suffer from stomachache.

If the top of your nose is red, it may mean stress. You shouldn't eat chocolate or drink alcohol if you have a lot of stress. Try deep breathing instead.

CHIN The chin area is connected to the kidney and bladder. If the skin around the chin and mouth is dark, this may show problems with the kidneys or bladder.

RIGHT CHEEK Your right cheek is connected to the lung. If you have skin problems on your right cheek, this might mean illness in the lung. If your right cheek is a little red, it may be that you are getting a cold.

LEFT CHEEK Your left cheek is connected to the liver. If you are red on your left cheek and next to your nose, you may have a problem with your liver. Problems in this part of the face can also show emotional illness, such as anger and depression, because the liver network is connected to the nervous system.

Speaking

1 Work in groups. Which is most important to health? Rank in order.

- don't drink alcohol ....
- eat good food ....
- don't drink fizzy drinks ....
- have good relationships ....
- don't eat junk food ....
- have regular check-ups ....
- don't smoke ....
- manage stress ....
- don't watch TV ....
- sleep well ....
- take regular exercise ....
- take vitamins ....

2 Compare your order with another group. Explain your reasons for the order. Work together to agree on a new order.

You should sleep well and then you will feel good the next day, you won't want junk food and you will want to take exercise. So it's number one!

6.4 Functional language: advice

Tune in

1 Work in pairs. Look at the photos. What is the situation? Why is it stressful?

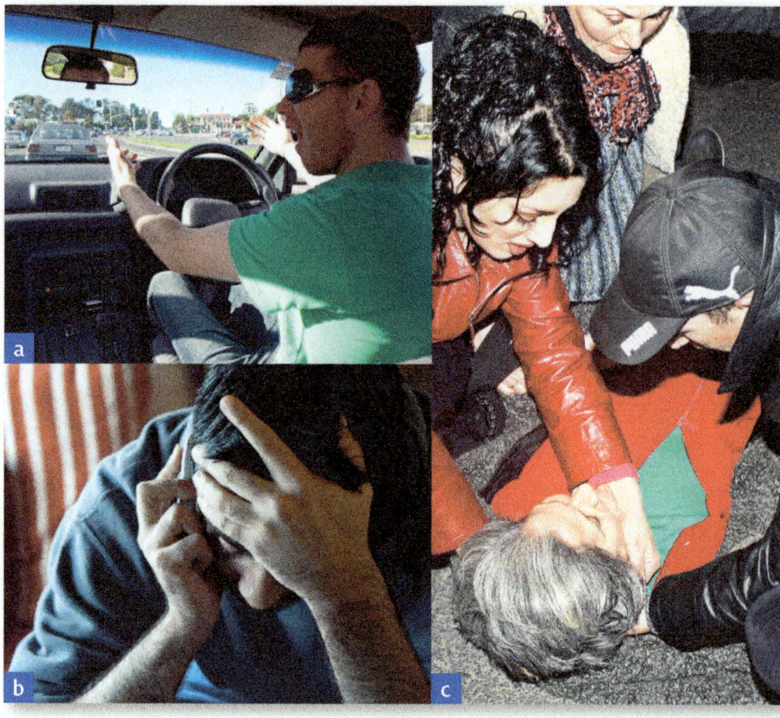

2 a 6.10 Listen. Which three conversations go with the photos?

b Listen again. Match each of the six situations to a piece of advice.

1	....	a	Call the emergency number.
2	....	b	Go home and go to bed.
3	....	c	Call and let someone know.
4	....	d	Ask someone for help.
5	....	e	Call a doctor.
6	....	f	Talk to a professional.

Focus on language

3 Listen again and complete the phrases.

1 Why .... go home and go to bed?
2 You .... call the emergency number.
3 What .... I do?
4 Why .... speak to your teacher?
5 Do .... I should talk to my boss?
6 What .... calling your friend?
7 You .... call a doctor.

4 Work in groups. Discuss whether you agree with the advice they gave.

5 Complete this table of ways to ask for and give advice. Use the phrases in 3 to help you.

Asking for advice	Giving advice
What .... I do?	You ....
Do you think I .... ?	You shouldn't ....
	Why .... you... ?
	What .... ?
	You .... to...

Notice *advice*

The noun *advice* is uncountable.
We can't say *He gave me some ~~advices~~*.
We can say *a piece of advice*.
This is countable.
My mother gave me two pieces of advice.

Over to you

6 Work in groups. Look at the photos. What problems can you see here?

7 Make notes on what advice you could give.

8 Take turns to ask for advice and to give advice for each photo.

Writing task: A formal email

Tune in

1 Read the email from a teacher to a funding agency (an organisation that gives money). What is the teacher asking for?

To: request@edufund.co.uk
From: bmarshall@WestleaCS.edu

I am a teacher at a school in London. I am a new teacher to the school and we do not have enough money for all the things we need.

Teaching English literature to teenagers is an interesting task because they often enjoy writing and they have great stories to tell. I have found that they become very interested in stories about young people like themselves who go through a lot of problems.

I would like them to have their own copies of *Romeo and Juliet* and 30 books for my students would cost £289.

I would be delighted if you could help us with this.

Thank you very much.

Brad Marshall

2 Read the email again. Answer the questions.

1 Where does he work?
2 What does he teach?
3 Why does he like teaching teenagers?
4 How many books does he want?

3 Imagine you work for the funding agency. You have twenty people a day who ask for money and you have £500 a day to give away. Should you give the money to this teacher? Why/Why not?

Prepare for task

4 Work in pairs. Read about the different organisations. Imagine you work for a funding agency that wants to donate some money. Which one would you give money to and why? How much money would you give?

Teens in Need is an organisation that works with homeless young people. We go out on the streets and give them the help they need to stay clean and safe and help them to plan their future.

Save the Animals is an organisation that protects animals from cruelty and extinction in different parts of our planet.

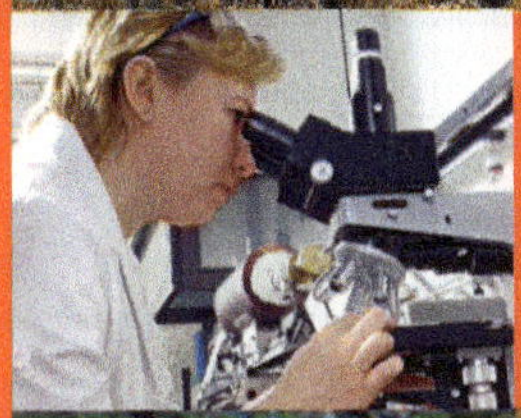

Research Doctors is a group of doctors who are looking for a cure for HIV/AIDS. The money you donate gives hope to millions of people in all parts of the world.

Girls First supports young women around the world by giving them access to education. Your money helps to pay for a young woman's education.

Planet in Danger helps you to help the environment by educating people about ways to clean and protect our world.

Task

5 Work in groups of three. Choose a local organisation (e.g. a school or hospital in your hometown). Write an email to a funding agency. Say

1 who you are.
2 what the money is for. Describe the organisation and why it needs money.
3 how much money you need.

6 **a** Read other groups' emails. Choose one you would like to give the money to and say why.

b Think about how much money they need, if it is a good cause and how it will help.

Report back

7 Tell the others in the class which organisation you chose to give money to and why.

→ Go to Review B, Unit 6, p. 70

VOCABULARY

Life stages

1 Write the name of a person you know who

- got a new job this year.
- was born before 1970.
- has got married.
- has gone to university.

2 Work in pairs. Ask and answer the questions.

- How do you know the people in 1? (e.g. friend, aunt, grandmother)
- How old are they?
- How often do you see them?

Activities

3 a Complete the table with the activities.

computer games crafts fishing football karate skateboarding

do	go	play
....	....	....
....	....	....

b Work in pairs. Which ones a) do you do? b) do your friends do?

Home life

4 a Choose the correct words to complete the sentences.

1 My mum never *does / makes* the housework.
2 I prefer to *bring / do* the shopping online.
3 I often look *after / for* my sister's children.
4 I *make / do* dinner for the family every night.
5 We usually *pay / spend* our bills online.

b Work in pairs. Are the sentences true for you? What is the same/different?

GRAMMAR

Present perfect & past simple

1 a Complete the text using the correct form of the verbs.

(1) .... you ever .... *(read)* any of the *Twilight* books by Stephenie Meyer? (2) .... you ever *(see)* any of the films? Stephenie Meyer (3) .... *(wrote)* her first novel about a girl, Bella, who meets her vampire boyfriend in the town of Forks, USA. It (4) .... *(become)* a best-selling novel in 2005. Since that time, the town of Forks (5) .... *(change)* completely. In 2009, over 8,000 people (6) .... *(visit)* the town. In the same year, many new shops and restaurants (7) .... *(open)*. Since *Twilight*, sales in the town centre (8) .... *(grow)* by nearly 1,000%!

b Work in pairs. Do you know any places which have changed? Tell your partner about them.

Present perfect with *for* & *since*

2 Complete the sentences with your own ideas. Add one more sentence about yourself with *for* or *since*.

- I have lived in this town since ....
- I have known the teacher of this class for ....
- I have had this hairstyle since ....
- I haven't been to the cinema for ....

Comparatives & superlatives

3 Write six sentences about people in your family. Use comparatives and superlatives.

1 old
2 difficult
3 easy
4 young
5 busy
6 small
7 interesting
8 good at cooking

young – The youngest person in my family is Faustina. She's only two!

FUNCTIONAL LANGUAGE

Catching up

1 a Complete the sentences with the words in the box.

back going missed see soon tell

1 We must meet up again ....
2 I've got lots to .... you.
3 It's great to .... you again.
4 Welcome ....
5 I've .... you.
6 How's it .... ?

b R5 Listen and check. Then choose one of the sentences and continue the conversation.

LOOKING BACK

- How many people live in your home? Can you describe them using language from this unit?
- Are you similar to your family? Compare yourself to a member of your family.
- Have you ever had an experience similar to a person in this unit? What happened? How did you feel?

VOCABULARY

Education & learning

1 Add as many words as you can to the word maps.

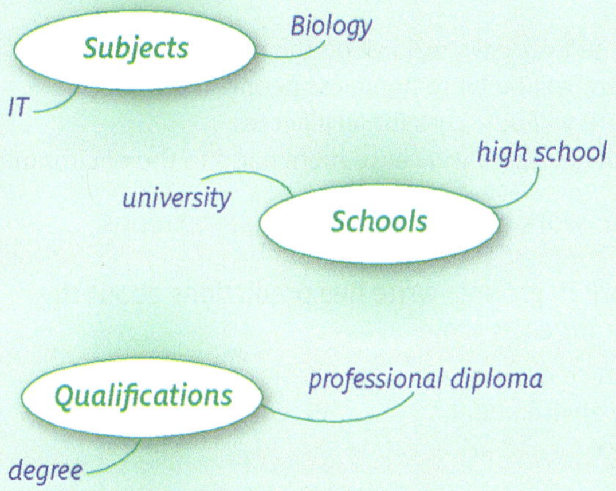

2 Take turns to describe three words from 1. Can you guess which words your partner is describing?

'2 + 2.' 'Is it Maths?'
'Study of plants and animals.' 'Is it Biology?'

-ed/-ing adjectives

3 Choose the correct words. Complete the sentences with your ideas.

1 .... is a really *fascinated / fascinating* subject.
2 I felt *pleased / pleasing* when ....
3 One of the most *interested / interesting* things I've done is ....
4 I usually feel *tired / tiring* when ....
5 I think my .... is *confused / confusing* because ....

Adjectives + prepositions

4 Match adjectives 1–6 to prepositions a–f.

1 bored	a about
2 different	b at
3 excited	c from
4 good	d in
5 interested	e with
6 similar	f to

5 **a** Choose four adjectives + prepositions from 4. Use them in four different sentences about people or things connected with school.

Mrs Green is different from my other teachers. Her lessons are really funny!

b Work in pairs. Compare your sentences. Explain why these things or people are important to you.

GRAMMAR

Present continuous & *going to*

1 **a** Fill in the diary with your plans for the weekend.

Saturday	*morning*	
	afternoon	
	evening	
Sunday	*morning*	
	afternoon	
	evening	

b Work in pairs. Tell your partner about your plans. Use the present continuous and *going to*.

Must & have to

2 **a** Complete the sentences with *must*, *mustn't*, *have to* or *don't have to* so that they're true for your country.

1 All children .... go to school.
2 Most school students .... wear a uniform.
3 Students .... stay at school until they're 16.
4 University students .... study for three years.
5 Primary school students .... study English.

b Work in groups. Discuss the sentences. Do you agree with the statements?

FUNCTIONAL LANGUAGE

Sounding polite

1 Write the requests more politely.

1 Tell me your address.
2 Lend me your pen.
3 Help me with my homework.
4 Tell me the answers to the exercises on this page.
5 Come for a coffee with me.

2 R6 Listen and compare your answers. Then act out the conversations with your partner.

LOOKING BACK

- What was your last English lesson like? What was the most interesting thing you learnt?
- What must you do tonight? What else are you going to do?
- Do you have to go to school or work tomorrow? What are you going to do there?

VOCABULARY

Help

1 **a** Complete the jobs and services.

1 ambulance ....
2 charity ....
3 emergency ....
4 police ....
5 help ....
6 fire ....

b Which do you think is the most important? Why?

2 **a** Work in pairs. How many root words can you think of that take the suffix a) *-ful*? b) *-less*?

b Join another pair. Compare your answers. How many words do you have in total?

Senses

3 **a** Which verbs of senses 1–5 do we usually use to talk about the things in the box?

clothes and haircuts	food	music	people

1 taste 2 feel 3 look 4 sound 5 smell

b Use an adjective to describe an example of each thing in 3a.

food – Chocolate cake tastes really great.

Health problems

4 **a** What advice could you give people with these problems?

1 I have a headache.
2 My throat hurts.
3 My tooth hurts.
4 I hurt my arm in an accident.

b Work in pairs. Put the sentences in order (1 = most serious, 4 = least serious). Does your partner agree with your order?

GRAMMAR

Modal verbs: *can/can't, should/shouldn't*

1 **a** Write the words in order to make questions.

1 rich more people poor give money people to Should ?
2 young Can find people country in your work ?
3 work shouldn't people fewer Why hours ?

b Work in groups. Ask and answer the questions.

Modal verbs: *will, may, might*

2 **a** Change the sentences using the words in the box so that the sentences express your personal opinion.

I don't think	I think	may	might	not

1 In the future we will live on the moon.
2 There will be more homeless people in the world.
3 There will be a cure for all illnesses.
4 Rich countries will cause more harm to the environment.

b Work in groups. Discuss your opinions.

3 **a** Work in groups. Write five predictions about the future for each topic.

1 medicine
2 the environment
3 work
4 health
5 education

b Swap your predictions with another group. Put the other group's ideas in order from *most likely to happen* to *least likely to happen*.

FUNCTIONAL LANGUAGE

Advice

1 **a** Read the pieces of advice. What do you think the problems were?

1 You should go back and ask her to fix it. It looks awful.
2 I'll help you. Why don't you ask a couple of other friends to come over and help too?
3 What about saying you're sorry to your dad? That should help.
4 You shouldn't go somewhere without a recommendation! Ask people, or you could look for a review online.
5 Call an ambulance immediately!

b R7 Listen and check. What other information did you hear?

2 Work in pairs. Give another piece of advice for each situation in 1a.

LOOKING BACK

- Which section in this unit did you find a) the most useful? b) the most interesting? Why?
- In this unit, which problem did you find the most serious or difficult? Why?
- Make a prediction about your English learning in the future and compare with your partner.

READING & SPEAKING

1 **a** Read the online post. How does Tadzio feel about his English exam?

From: *Tadzio89*	Hello! I'd like some advice. I've got a really important English exam next month. My friends seem quite relaxed about it, but I'm terrified. I'm having nightmares about it! Any ideas?

b Work in pairs. Discuss how you usually feel about tests and exams.

2 Read the replies. Who talks about

1 the month before the exam? 2 the night before the exam? 3 the day of the exam?

From: *erikhaakon*	Try revising with friends. You can test each other, practise your speaking – and have a bit of fun, too! But don't do this the night before the exam. You'll get too stressed!
From: *Easy_going_Alix*	Don't panic! You've got lots of time. You should write a study plan for the month before the exam. Give details. Don't just write 'English – all week' – that's scary! Write 'the present perfect, Friday, 6 p.m. to 7.30 p.m.' You'll be amazed how much you can learn in the time!
From: *Positive_thinker*	Nightmares? That's bad. Start looking at your notes now, and read them regularly. I use highlighter pens to colour the most important information – it helps me to remember it. I always use an orange highlighter pen. I read that orange is the best colour for thinking!
From: *Red_rose*	Don't do lots of revision in the evening before your exam. You should go to bed early.
From: *mjm556*	It's really important to stay calm in the exam. If you aren't sure about a question, don't panic! Give your best answer or just guess. And make sure you answer all of the questions. It's always better to write something than to write nothing.

3 **a** Read the replies again. What do you think are the best ideas?

b Work in pairs. Compare your ideas and choose the three best ideas.

WRITING

4 **a** Work in pairs. Write an 'exam tips' poster. Include the three headings in 2. Give at least two pieces of advice for each heading.

b Compare your posters with another pair. Add one more tip to their poster.

5 Work in groups. How many of the tips do you already do? What things are you going to try?

QUICK CHECK

Complete the checklist below.

Can you...	Yes, I can.	Yes, more or less.	I need to look again.
1 talk about your past experiences?	☐	☐	☐
2 compare people, places and things?	☐	☐	☐
3 talk about future plans?	☐	☐	☐
4 ask for information on the telephone?	☐	☐	☐
5 give advice?	☐	☐	☐
6 talk about your abilities?	☐	☐	☐
7 describe your feelings?	☐	☐	☐
8 talk about future possibilities?	☐	☐	☐

Compare your answers with a partner.

- What else do you know now after studying units 4–6?
- Do you need to look again at any of the sections?
- Do you need any extra help from your teacher?

UNIT 1 GRAMMAR REFERENCE

1.1 PRESENT SIMPLE & PRESENT CONTINUOUS

Present simple

+	I/You/We/They	understand		French.
	He/She/It	understand**s**		
–	I/You/We/They	don't	understand	Japanese.
	He/She/It	do**es**n't		

Use the present simple to talk about

1 general truths or situations *I live in São Paulo. Roberto works as a teacher.*

2 regular habits / routines *School starts at 6 a.m. every day. I usually get up at 8 a.m.*

Use time expressions like *usually*, *sometimes*, *never*, *always* and *often*.

Present continuous

+	I'm You're/We're/They're He's/She's/It's	reading.
–	I'm not You/We/They aren't He/She/It isn't	reading.

Use the present continuous to talk about actions that are happening at the moment. *We're reading our English book right now.*

Use time expressions like *at the moment*, *today* and *right now*.

Stative verbs

Stative verbs describe feelings, thoughts and sensations. We do not usually use these verbs in a continuous form. *I like this class.* NOT ~~*I'm liking*~~ *this class.*

Stative verbs include *be, like, love, hate, need, belong, know, want, believe, understand.*

▶ 1.1

1.2 QUESTIONS

Questions with the verb *to be*

The verb *to be* comes before the subject in both yes/no questions and *Wh-* questions. ***Are** you Canadian? **Was** he happy with his course? Where **is** your English school? Where **were** you yesterday?*

Yes/no questions with other verbs

The subject comes between the auxiliary verb and the main verb. In the present simple and past simple use *do, does* and *did* as the auxiliary verb.

Present simple			
Do	I/you/we/they	speak	French very well?
Does	he/she/it	understand	Japanese?
Past simple			
Did	I/you/we/they/he/she/it	understand	German?

Wh- questions with other verbs

In *Wh-* questions the question word comes at the beginning of the question followed by the auxiliary, the subject and the main verb.

Wh- ?	Auxiliary verb	Subject	Main verb	
What	are	you	studying	at the moment?
What	did	they	do	last night?
Where	does	he	go	to school?

▶ 1.2

1.1

a Read the sentences. Tick the ones that are correct and correct the ones that are not.

1 I usually play football on Sundays.
2 We are often watching TV in the evening.
3 I'm not understanding the words of English songs.
4 I'm learning French at the moment.
5 We eat dinner right now.
6 I'm not really liking sports.

b Are any of these sentences true for you?

c Complete the conversation with the present simple or present continuous.

MARSHA Where .... you ....? *(go)*
TIM I .... *(go)* to my yoga class. I always .... *(do)* yoga on Mondays.
MARSHA What time .... the class ....? *(start)*
TIM It .... *(start)* at 6 p.m. and .... *(finish)* at 7.30. .... you .... *(want)* to come?
MARSHA No, thanks. I .... *(do)* my homework. I .... *(not like)* to do homework late at night.
TIM OK, I'll see you later.

1.2

a Write the words in the correct order to form questions.

1 musical instrument you play Do a ?
2 sport do do How often you ?
3 have you favourite a Do TV show ?
4 exam you for Are an studying at the moment ?
5 last What you night did do ?

b Answer the questions. Use full sentences.

c Write the questions for the answers.

1 ....
I live in New York City.
2 ....
No, I'm single.
3 ....
I'm working on a film about a person with an unusual hobby.
4 ....
My last film was about a person who lives in Thailand.
5 ....
I go to the cinema about twice a week.

2.1 Past simple

+	verb + *-ed* *	I/You/He/ She/It/We/ They	watched	the film.
–	*didn't* + infinitive	I/You/ He/She/It/ We/They	didn't watch	the film.
?	*did* + subject + infinitive	Did	I/you/he/she it/we/they	watch the film?

* Some verbs have an irregular form: *make → made, do → did, have → had, fly → flew, sleep → slept, take → took, eat → ate.*

Use the past simple to talk about completed past actions and past situations.

The Tate Modern opened in 2000.
I lived in a small flat in Barcelona five years ago.

Past simple time expressions

Use time expressions like

in 2007, last week, last night, last year, ago, yesterday, on Tuesday, in January, an hour ago, when, at 8.30.

▶ 2.1

2.2 Past continuous

+	I/He/She/It You/We/They	was were	eating.
–	I/He/She/It You/We/They	was not (wasn't) were not (weren't)	eating.
?	Was Were	I/he/she/it you/we/they	eating?

Use the past continuous to talk about an action in progress at a certain time in the past.

I was walking home at 5.30 this afternoon.
My friends were waiting outside the restaurant.

▶ 2.2

2.3 Past simple & past continuous

Use the past continuous to show that one action was in progress when another, shorter action took place.

I ***was putting*** *the tent up when I* ***heard*** *a strange noise.*

We often use *while* + past continuous.

I took a photo of the zebra ***while*** *it was eating.*

Use two past simple verbs to show that one action followed the other.

I ***heard*** *a strange noise and* ***looked up*** *to see what it was.*

We often use *and, then* and *so* to link the two actions.

I finished putting up the tent ***then*** *I went to park the car.*

NOTE: We do not usually use stative verbs in the continuous form.

I loved animals when I was a child. NOT *I ~~was loving~~ animals when I was a child.*

(See also 1.1.)

▶ 2.3

2.1

a Read the text about Bear Grylls. Look at the verbs in italics. Find and correct five mistakes.

> Bear Grylls *learned* to swim and climb when he *were* very young. When he *finished* school, he *spended* some time hiking in the Himalayas before he *joined* the Army. In 2000 he *rode* around the UK on a jet ski. Three years later he *cross* the Atlantic. In 2008 he *went* on an expedition to climb the highest peak in Antarctica but he *didn't completed* his mission because he *breaked* his shoulder. But this *didn't stop* him and two years later he was back again, trying to break yet another record!

b What else can you remember about Bear Grylls from the lesson? Write three sentences about his adventures. Then check your answers on page 17.

2.2

a Look at the picture. It shows a party that took place at João's flat last night. What were the people doing? Write six sentences using the verbs in the box.

choose	dance	eat	play	read	watch

b Write three more sentences explaining what they <u>weren't</u> doing.

2.3

a Complete the text using the past simple or the past continuous form of the verbs in brackets.

It was a beautiful day. The sun (1) .... (*shine*) and the sky was blue. We (2) .... (*cycle*) along a quiet road in the countryside when we (3) .... (*heard*) some dogs. But they were very far away so we (4) .... (*not/think*) any more about it and (5) .... (*continue*) on our ride. We (6) .... (*just/come*) round a corner in the road when suddenly an enormous white dog (7) .... (*jump*) out in front of us. Three other dogs (8) .... (*follow*) him. They were wild dogs and we were scared. We (9) .... (*throw*) sticks and rocks at them. Eventually they (10) .... (*ran*) away.

UNIT 3 GRAMMAR REFERENCE

3.1 Relative clauses

Use relative clauses when you want to give more information about a person or thing.

— Who's that?
*— Oh, he's the guy **who painted our house**.*

Relative pronouns

Relative pronoun	Refers to
who	person
which	thing
that	people and things

Main clauses and relative clauses

When we use relative clauses the sentence has two parts.

Main clause	Relative clause
This is the person	**who** lives next door to me.
Have you seen the film	**that** won the Oscar this year?

▶ 3.1

3.2 Articles: *a/an*, *the*, no article

A, *an* (indefinite article)

Use *a* and *an* to talk about single objects without referring to a specific object.

*Do you have **a** pencil?* (I'm interested in one pencil, but I don't mind which pencil it is)

We use *a/an* with singular countable nouns. We use *a* before a consonant and *an* before a vowel sound.

*I think I need **a** new phone.*
*Can I have **an** apple?*

Note: not all words that are written with a vowel start with a vowel sound.

university /ˌjuːnɪ'vɜːsɪtɪ/ *He went to **a** university in the States.*
European /ˌjʊərə'pɪən/ *I've got **a** European passport.*
euro /'jʊːrəʊ/ *Can you give me **a** euro?*

The (definite article)

Use *the* to refer to a specific person or thing.

*Can I have **the** pencil I gave you?* (= a specific pencil)

We also use *the* when there is only one in the context.

***The** boss isn't very happy today.* (there's only one boss)

We use *the* before

- uncountable nouns *I love **the** coffee your mother makes.*
- singular countable nouns ***The** computer I use at work is really slow.*
- plural countable nouns *They put **the** logos on the front page.*

No article

Don't use an article before singular or plural nouns when we are referring to people or things in general.

I like old buildings.
I visited temples in Thailand.

▶ 3.2

3.1

a Read the sentences. Cross out any unnecessary words.

1 Kim introduced me to the man who he is going to be our teacher next year.
2 I love that coffee shop that you took me to it last week.
3 Can you tell me some more about that film which you saw it last night?
4 Your brother is probably the funniest person that I've ever met him.

b Use *who* or *which* to join the two sentences. Remember to drop any unnecessary pronouns.

1 This is the photo. I took it last year on holiday.
2 These are the people. We met them at the hotel.
3 This is the hotel. It was in the centre of town.
4 This was my favourite bar. We visited it every night!

c Match the photo to one of the sentences in **b**. Think of one or two holiday photos that you have taken. Write sentences with *who* or *which* to describe the photos.

3.2

a Choose the correct article to complete the conversation.

A My favourite sign is (1)*the/a* sign for (2)*the/a* fire escape. Have you seen it?
B Which one?
A The sign they put up on (3)*the* / - side of (4)*a/the* building for example. You know, there's (5)*a/the* little man and he's running as fast as he can away from (6) *the*/ - fire.
B I love (7)*an/the* old-fashioned sign for roadworks. You know (8)*a/the* little man with his spade, he's digging (9)*a/an* hole or something, but it looks more like he's opening (10)*a/an* umbrella.

A I know (11)*the/-* sign you mean.

b Complete the description of this sign using *a/an*, *the* or no article (-).

A This sign shows (1) .... children crossing (2) .... road. I like (3) .... way they are walking so slowly and seriously. (4) .... children I know don't look like that!
B I don't think it's two children. It's (5) .... girl and her mother. But I don't know what they're carrying! They don't look like (6) .... schoolbags to me!
A No it looks more like (7) .... handbag.

4.1 PRESENT PERFECT

Form the present perfect with *have/has ('ve/has)* + past participle.
Regular past participles end in *-ed*. Many verbs have irregular past participles.

+	I/You/We/They He/She/It	have has	eaten.
–	I/You/We/They He/She/It	haven't hasn't	eaten.
?	Have Has	I/you/we/they he/she/It	eaten?

Use the present perfect to talk about past experiences in a general way without saying exactly when those experiences took place.

I've tried it before. (at some time in the past, but it isn't important when)

Time expressions

We often use *ever* with question forms and *never* with negative forms.

*Have you **ever** been to New York? I've **never** visited the National Museum.*

▶ 4.1

4.2 PRESENT PERFECT & PAST SIMPLE

Use both the present perfect and the past simple to talk about actions in the past. Use the present perfect when you are more interested in the action than the time it happened.

They've found him.

Use the past simple to talk about when and where an action or event happened. We often use time expressions like *yesterday*, *ago*, *last*.

They found him in Oxford two months ago.

Present perfect + *for/since*

Use the present perfect with *for* to talk about a period of time that continues into the present.

I've lived here for six years.

Use the present perfect with *since* to talk about when an action or situation started. The action or situation continues into the present.

I've lived here since 2005.

▶ 4.2

4.3 COMPARATIVES & SUPERLATIVES

Use comparative and superlative forms of adjectives to compare two or more things or people.

We normally use comparatives to compare two things, or two groups of things. Form a comparative adjective with adjective + *-er* or *more* + adjective. We use *than* to link the two parts of the comparison.

Moscow is bigger than Paris. Kids are more creative than adults.

Use superlatives to talk about a person or thing that has more of a certain quality than others of their type. Form a superlative adjective with adjective + *-est* or *most* + adjective. We often use *the* or a possessive adjective with superlative adjectives.

Sara is my oldest friend. Nico's the most patient teacher I know.

SPELLING: With a small group of one-syllable adjectives you need to double the final consonant and then add *-er* or *-est*. These adjectives end in a consonant-vowel-consonant combination and include:
hot → hotter → hottest, big → bigger → biggest,
fat → fatter → fattest, red → redder → reddest,
thin → thinner → thinnest, sad → sadder → saddest

▶ 4.3

4.1

a Complete the conversations using the present perfect form of the verb in brackets and short answers.

1 A (1) .... *(you/ever/do)* any belly-dancing?
B No, I (2) .... , but I'd love to. And you?
A Yes, I (3) .... , I (4) .... *(just/start)* classes at the gym. You should try. You'd love it!

2 A I (5) .... *(always/want)* to try kite-surfing.
B Really? I (6) .... *(not try)* , but my brother (7) .... *(do)* it. He's really good at it.
A (8) .... *(he/try)* paragliding as well?
B No, he (9) .... , he's too scared!

b Re-write the conversations for people you know, using new activities.

4.2

a Read the sentences. Tick the ones that are correct and correct the ones that are not.

1 We didn't play tennis since May.
2 They've lived in Tokyo for two years.
3 That's a nice dress. How long did you have it?
4 I've forgotten the name of the film.
5 I didn't finish the homework yesterday.

b Complete the sentences with *for* or *since*.

1 They've been married .... 15 years.
2 Peter has worked at the bookstore .... 2007.
3 He's been in a meeting .... 11 o'clock.
4 I've had my car .... 18 months.

c Underline the time expressions in the sentences in b. Write sentences that are true for you using the present perfect.

4.3

a Look at the table about three Australian cities. Complete the sentences with the comparative or superlative form of the adjectives in brackets. Add *than* and *the* where necessary.

	Sydney	Melbourne	Perth
Population	4 million	3.5 million	1.5 million
Average temperature January	26°	27.2°	31°
Average annual rainfall	1200 mm	650 mm	790 mm
Average house price	$250,000	$225,000	$495,000

1 The population of Melbourne is .... than the population of Perth, but Sydney has .... population. *(big)*
2 Melbourne is .... Sydney, but Perth is .... *(hot)*
3 Melbourne is .... city, but Perth is .... Sydney. *(dry)*
4 Houses in Perth are .... , and houses in Sydney are .... than in Melbourne. *(expensive)*

b Write four sentences comparing three cities in your country.

5.1 PRESENT CONTINUOUS & *GOING TO*

Present continuous

Use the present continuous to talk about things that are happening now. (See 1.1.)

We can also use the present continuous to talk about the future. Use the present continuous to talk about fixed plans for the future, often with a time or place.

I'm meeting Joan for dinner this weekend. (= I've arranged this)

Going to

Use *going to* with the verb *to be* and the infinitive.

+	I'm You/We/They're He/She/It's	going to	start a new course.
–	I'm not You/We/They aren't He/She/It isn't	going to	start a new course.
?	Am I Are you/we/they Is he/she/it	going to	start a new course?

We can also use *going to* to talk about plans for the future. We don't need to give a specific time.

We're going to buy a house (one day). (= a general plan)

In some cases, we can use both forms without changing the meaning.

I'm cooking dinner this evening. I'm going to cook dinner this evening.

In other cases, there is a clear difference in meaning.

We're going to get married (one day). (= a general plan)

We're getting married next March. (= it is arranged)

NOTE: We normally don't repeat *to go*.

They're going to the cinema. NOT *They're going ~~to go~~ to the cinema.*

▶ 5.1

5.2 *MUST(N'T)* & *(DON'T) HAVE TO* FOR OBLIGATION

Must & *have/has to*

Must is a modal auxiliary verb. It follows these rules of form:

1 use *must* + infinitive without ~~*to*~~
2 use *must* to form questions and negatives.
Must you do that right now? I mustn't be late.
3 you don't need an *-s* for the third person singular.
He must report to the director's office immediately.

Use *must* and *have/has to* to talk about rules and obligations.

I must/have to be at the office by nine. I must/have to work this evening.

NOTE: *must* is not often used in question forms. *Do I have to?* is more common. *Do I have to call her?* NOT *~~Must~~ I call her?*

Mustn't & *don't/doesn't have to*

Use *mustn't* to say that it is important NOT to do something, or that something is against the rules.

You mustn't eat or drink near the computers. (= do not do this)

Use *don't/doesn't have to* to say that it is not necessary or obligatory to do something, you are free to choose.

You don't have to bring your own laptop. (= this is not necessary but you can do it if you want to)

▶ 5.2

5.1

a Look at the calendar for three flatmates. Write sentences about their future plans. Use the present continuous.

	Pablo	Krista	John
Monday		(1) 8 p.m. – dinner with Mum & Dad	
Tuesday			(2) 2 p.m. – Spanish exam
Wednesday	(3) 10 a.m. – dentist		
Thursday		(4) 1 p.m. – shopping w/Dana	
Friday			(5) 7.30 p.m. cinema
Saturday	(6) 9 a.m. – football semi finals		
Sunday			

b Complete the sentences with *going to* and a verb of your choice.

1 Hey, it's your birthday on Saturday! What are you going to do?
I ....
2 Marco, you know smoking is really bad for you.
Yes, I know, I .... , I promise!
3 Are you going on holiday this year?
No, I don't have enough money. I ....
4 Is Krassy coming to see the film with us tonight?
No, I think he ....

c Think of three things you are going to do next weekend. Write three full sentences.

5.2

a Complete the sentences using *must*, *have to*, *don't have to* and *mustn't*. Sometimes more than one answer is possible.

must (x2) mustn't have to don't have to (x2)

1 You really .... study harder if you want to pass the exam.
2 This isn't a direct train to Brussels. You .... change at the next station.
3 My brother's band are playing at the park tonight. The concert's free. You .... pay.
4 I really .... remember to call Mum this evening. I forgot yesterday!
5 We can't have the meeting on Friday. Friday's a bank holiday so we .... go to work.
6 I'm really sorry, but you do know that you .... smoke in the office, don't you?

b Look at the sentences again. Who do you think each person is speaking to? Where are they?

6.1 Modal verbs: *can/can't, should/shouldn't*

Can, should, will, may and *might* are modal auxiliary verbs. Use modal auxiliary verbs to add information about the speaker's attitude to the main verb.

I don't swim. (This tells us a fact.)

I can't swim. (This adds information about the person's ability.)

All modal verbs follow these rules of form (see also 5.2):

1 use the modal + infinitive without ~~to~~

2 use the modal to form questions and negatives

Can you speak Chinese? I might not come tonight.

3 you don't need an *s* for the third person singular

He should see a doctor. She can't see you right now.

+	I/ You/He/She/It/We/They	can	paint.
–	I/You/He/She/It/We/They	can't	paint.
?	Can	I/you/he/she/it/we/they	paint?

Can/Can't

Meaning	Example
to have the ability	*I can play the piano.*
not to have the ability	*She can't speak French.*
something is possible or allowed	*I can go to the party tomorrow.*
something is not possible or not allowed	*We can't stay very long because I need to get home early.*

Should/Shouldn't

Meaning	Example
something is a good idea	*You should do more exercise.*
something is a bad idea	*You shouldn't eat so many sweets.*

▶ 6.1

6.2 Predictions: *will, may, might*

sure – yes	*She will be there tomorrow.*
perhaps – yes	*She might be there tomorrow.* *She may be there tomorrow.*
perhaps – no	*She might not be there tomorrow.* *She may not be there tomorrow.*
sure – no	*She won't be there tomorrow.*

Use *will, might* and *may* to make predictions about the future.

Use *will* to say that we are **sure** something will happen.

Use *might* or *may* to say that we **think** something is **possible** but we're not sure.

She'll give you some ideas. (I'm sure this is true.)

She might/may give you some ideas. (This is a possibility, but I'm not 100% sure.)

When we want to ask other people what their opinion is about the future we usually use *will*.

Will his father help him? What will he do?

▶ 6.2

6.1

a Look at the signs and complete sentences 1–6.

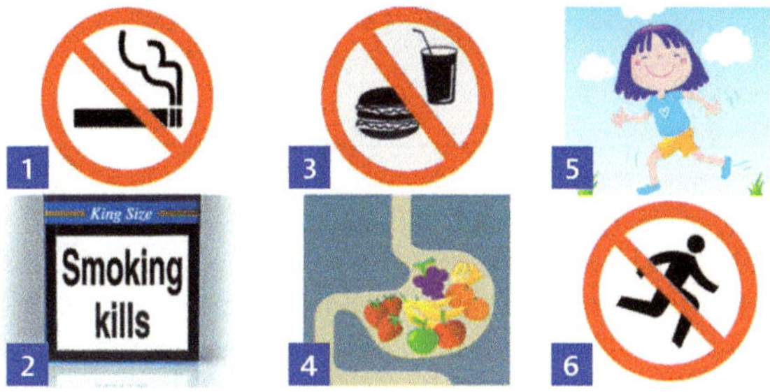

1 You .... smoke here.
2 You .... smoke.
3 You .... eat here.
4 You .... eat more fruit.
5 You .... do more exercise.
6 You .... run here.

b Complete the conversations with the best modal verb, *can, can't, should* or *shouldn't*.

JANIE Mum, (1) .... I go to Solmaz's party on Saturday?
MUM No, you (2) .... You're too young.

DOCTOR Hmm. You (3) .... try to eat less, because you need to lose some weight.
PATIENT OK. (4) .... I still eat cakes?
DOCTOR Well, you (5) .... eat a cake now and again, but you (6) .... eat one every day.

6.2

a Choose the most suitable explanation (a–c) for sentences 1–3.

1 If it doesn't rain this weekend, we're going to go camping.
 a We won't go camping.
 b We might not go camping.
 c We will go camping.

2 Tariq is not going to the meeting.
 a He won't be at the meeting.
 b He may not be at the meeting.
 c He'll be at the meeting.

3 Rachel and Xiaofan are going to win the contest.
 a They might not win the contest.
 b They may win the contest.
 c They'll win the contest.

b Complete the text using *will, won't, might* or *might not*.

Dario and Lina are six years old. They (1) .... leave school for at least another ten years. What (2) .... the world be like when they do? (3) .... their university courses be online? What languages (4) .... they need to know? They (5) .... want to study. They (6) .... want to do something else instead. But what? What jobs (7) .... be on offer? The same ones as today? Who knows! We (8) .... just have to wait and see.

c Write three sentences describing any changes that you think might take place in the next ten years.

1 LEARNING JOURNALS

a

Learning Journal

Date:

13th September 2011

Lesson:

Page: 4–5 (Speaking the same language)

What we did:

We talked about languages and countries. We listened to people from Paraguay and Wales talking about languages.

What I learned:

'first/second/official language', 'mother tongue', 'bilingual'

In class I was:

very nervous about speaking in English. ☹

For homework I'm going to do:

the vocabulary exercises in the Workbook

I'd also like to:

learn more about Paraguay. Try the Simple English Wikipedia?

b

13/09/11 (p4-5)

Vocab

first } language — Italian is my first language.
second } language
official } language — English is an official language in India.
bilingual — Stefan is bilingual. He speaks Spanish and Portuguese.
mother tongue — *What does this mean? Check in next lesson!*

Country	Languages
Wales	Welsh, English
Paraguay	Spanish, Guaraní
Holland	Dutch
China	Mandarin, Cantonese

Homework – Wbook vocab exercises

1 Read the journal entries. Which do you find easier to read? Which gives you most information about the lesson?

2 Read the journal entries again. Which entry includes

1 the activities the student did in the lesson?
2 the student's feelings about the lesson?
3 the page in the course book the lesson comes from?
4 example sentences for new vocabulary?
5 questions about vocabulary or grammar?
6 information about the homework?
7 ideas for extra study at home?

3 a Work in pairs. Read the advantages of writing a learning journal. Put the advantages in order, 1–8 (1 is the most important).

a You have to think about your lesson again.
b You can read your journal before a test.
c You can compare journals with a partner.
d You can see your progress.
e You can see which techniques help you to learn.
f You can record vocabulary that isn't in your course book.
g You can remember questions to ask your teacher.
h You practise writing in English.

b Can you think of any other advantages? Share your ideas with the class.

4 Write a journal entry about your last English lesson. Include:

- what you studied
- your feelings about the lesson
- any questions you have about the lesson
- what you will study at home

5 Work in pairs. Compare your journal entries. Are they similar or different?

TIP

Writing a learning journal is a useful way to remember what you have learned and to practise writing in English. You don't need to write full sentences. You just need to make sure you include the important information from your lesson.

2 COMMENTS ON A WEBSITE

1 Look at the comments. Which comment(s) come(s) from

1 a photo sharing website?
2 a social networking website?
3 a video sharing website?
4 a blog?

2 Work in pairs. Do you ever write comments like these? Where do you write them? Compare your answers with your partner.

3 Read the comments again. Find abbreviations that mean

1 congratulations
2 favourite
3 laugh out loud

4 **a** What does the writer omit in each comment? Match omitted words 1–4 to comments a–d.

1 I	a Very happy for you.
2 It's	b Looks like you had a great time!
3 I'm	c So interesting to read about your experiences.
4 It	d Really love this video.

b Read three more comments. Cross out all the unnecessary words.

1 I love this photo. It looks like such a beautiful place!
2 Great video, great song! It's definitely the best one from the band's new album.
3 We're so excited to hear you're engaged! It's fantastic news. ☺

5 **a** Work in pairs. Choose three photos from this book. Write comments about them for a photo sharing website.

b Visit one of the websites in 1 and leave a comment.

TIP

Comments on websites are generally short and informal. When you write a comment on a website, use short sentences and abbreviations. Remember to use a friendly tone!

3 WRITING TO SAY SORRY

1 Read emails 1–3. Match the emails to photos a–c.

1

Dear Sanjay,
So sorry to hear that you didn't pass your test on Thursday. Better luck next time! I'm going to send you some money to help you with more lessons. Soon you can drive here and visit me!
Your auntie Gita x x x

2

To Louise and Karl,

Congratulations on your lovely news! Thank you so much for inviting us to the wedding. Unfortunately, I'm writing to let you know that we can't come. I'm afraid that we're going to be in Australia in June! We're really sorry that we can't come - we hope you have a fantastic day.

Love,
Xana

3

Subject:

Dear Passenger,
We are writing to tell you that, due to industrial action, your flight to Rotterdam tomorrow is cancelled. We apologise for any inconvenience this causes. Please see www.dutchair.nl or call 0920 885588 for more information.

Vera Pfennings,
Customer Services Director

a

b

c

2 Read the emails again. Which email(s)

1 give(s) bad news?
2 respond(s) to bad news?
3 say(s) thank you before saying sorry?
4 is/are sent to more than one person?
5 is the most informal?
6 is the most formal?

3 Complete the phrases from the emails.

a We are w.................... to tell you that...
b So sorry to h.................... that...
c I'm writing to l.................... you k.................... that...
d We a.................... for...
e I'm a.................... that...
f We're really s.................... that...

4 **a** Which of the phrases in 3 do we use to

1 give bad news?
2 respond to bad news?
3 say sorry?

b Which phrase is only used in formal writing?

5 Choose one of the situations below and write an email to say sorry. Use the expressions in 3 if appropriate.

1 A good friend failed some important exams (decide what kind of exam). Write an email to make him/her feel better (think of something positive that you can say).

2 An old friend has invited you to his/her house for a holiday. Write an email to him/her to say that you can't visit and explain why.

3 You are a member of a club (decide what kind of club). You can't attend club meetings anymore. Write an email to the club secretary to say sorry and explain why.

TIP

Remember to make your emails friendly and sympathetic. Imagine you are the person receiving the email and think about how you feel when you read it.

1.4 Functional language, page 12, Exercise 8

e towels
f bottle opener
g sink plug
h remote control

2.4 Functional language, page 22, Exercise 5a

Student A
You are the passenger. The weather is bad today and there are delays to all of the flights. When you check in, ask about the delays to your flight.

2.4 Functional language, page 22, Exercise 5b

Student A
You are the hotel receptionist. Because of work to renovate the hotel sports facilities, the swimming pool and gym are closed. There is a private sports club across the road which hotel guests can use free of charge. The club is open until 10pm.

3.0 Key Vocabulary, page 25, B

- a as a capital city
- b for an emperor
- c in memory of a loved one
- d as a religious monument
- e as a defence against invasion
- f to hold competitions
- g to bury the dead
- h to protect an important source of water

3.4 Functional language, page 32, Exercise 7

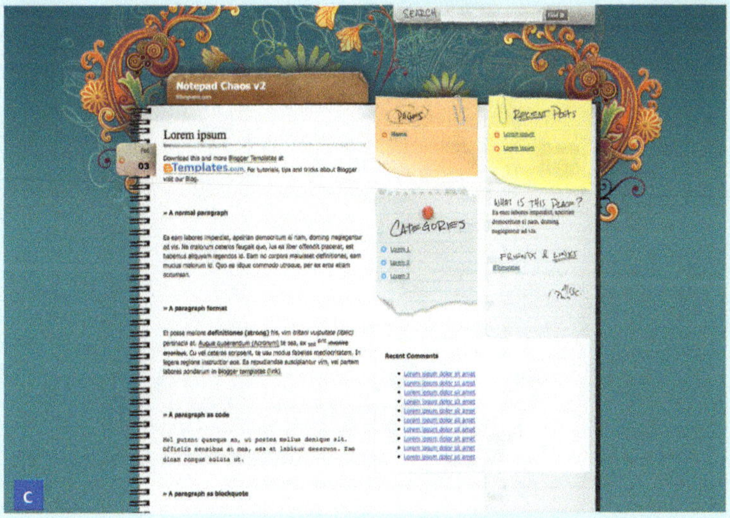

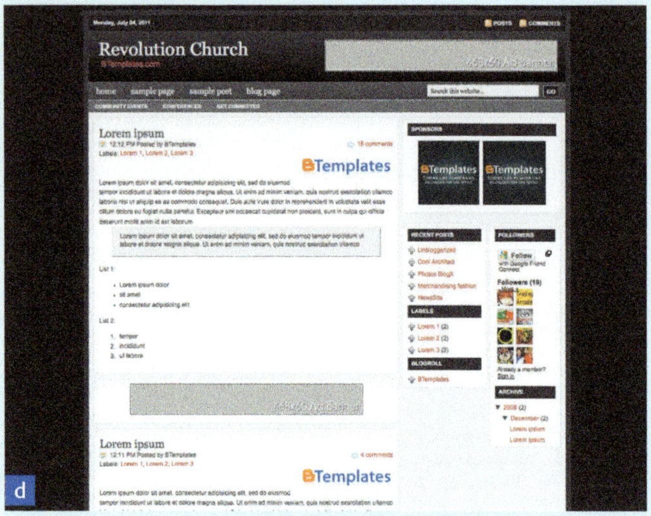

d

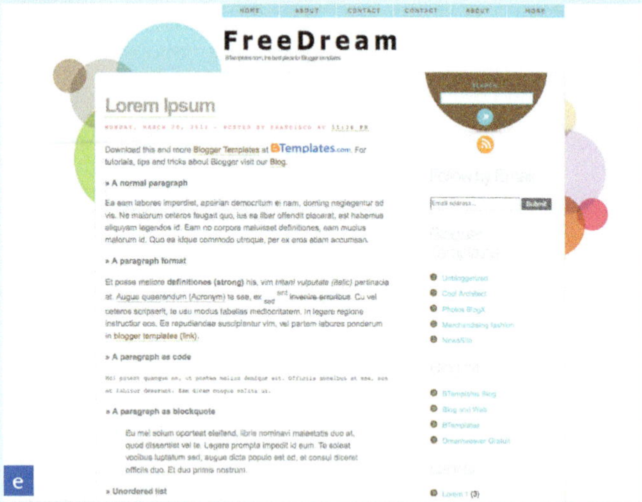

e

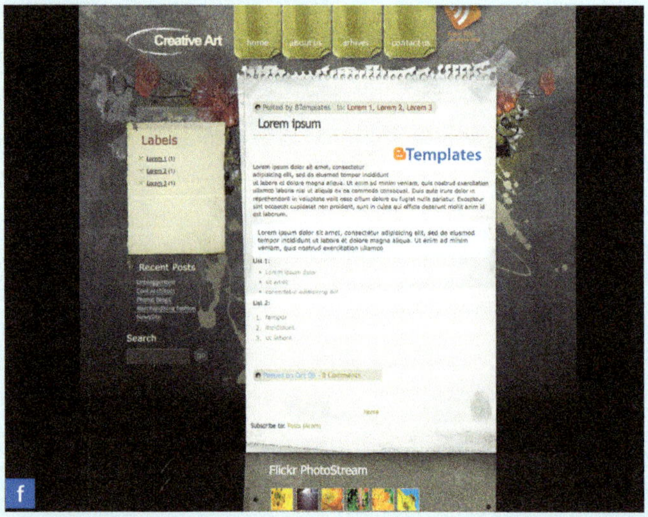

f

5.5 Speaking task, page 57, Exercise 4

Student A

Part 1

Read the information about the school in photo **a** and answer Student B's questions.

Name of school: City English	
1 Accommodation?	small, friendly hotel near Dublin (3 kilometres)
2 Courses – which subjects?	English, French, Spanish, Japanese
3 Class size?	1–5 students
4 Activities?	film club, trips around Dublin
5 Price?	€350

Part 2

Ask Student B questions to complete the table about the school in photo **c**.

Name of school: American Families	
1 Accommodation?	....
2 Courses – which subjects?	....
3 Class size?	....
4 Activities?	....
5 Price?	....

6.2 Vocabulary, page 62, Exercise 4

Student A

2.4 Functional language, page 22, Exercise 5a

Student B
You are the airline check-in assistant. The flight has been cancelled. All passengers are booked on to the next flight tomorrow morning. The airline has booked hotel rooms for all the passengers at the airport. They can get a free dinner at the hotel.

2.4 Functional language, page 22, Exercise 5b

Student B
You are the guest. You want to book in for two nights. You want to know the opening times of the swimming pool and gym.

5.5 Speaking task, page 57, Exercise 4

Student B

Part 1

Ask Student A questions to complete the table about the school in photo **a**.

Name of school: City English	
1 Accommodation?	....
2 Courses – which subjects?	....
3 Class size?	....
4 Activities?	....
5 Price?	....

Part 2

Read the information about the school in photo **c** and answer Student A's questions.

Name of school: American Families	
1 Accommodation?	students stay with American families in their homes
2 Courses – which subjects?	English, History, Literature
3 Class size?	10–15 students
4 Activities?	walks in the mountains, swimming, cycling
5 Price?	$550

6.2 Vocabulary, page 62, Exercise 4

Student B

8.2 Listening, page 86, Exercise 4b

1

Sue went to meet her birth family. She liked them and they liked her. The Millers were serious, shy people and so was Sue. She was never close to her brother Bob Mcdonald (who was not her real brother) and was worried that she would lose him.

2

Marti met her real brother (Bob McDonald) first and they became good friends because they were both outgoing and fun. She then met her birth parents, but Marti thought that they didn't want to get close to he, because they thought of Sue as their real daughter.

3

Marti was jealous because she thought she was losing her parents to Sue. Sue and Marti never became friends because they are very different and both felt jealous in some way. However, they now go to the family events of both families.

8.2 Reading, page 87, Exercise 3

He is a human chameleon, and because of this unique ability, he becomes the patient of a famous psychiatrist (Mia Farrow) who eventually falls in love with him – but not before he also becomes a psychiatrist himself, of course!

The film makes all this believable because it is very clever. It mixes real archive film of news reports from the 30s and 40s with new material that includes Allen. This is done using antique film cameras and lenses, which were made well before digital filmmaking technology made this easy. So, we see Allen superimposed next to real people (not actors!) from history. He even appears next to Charlie Chaplin!

So, who else does Zelig become in the film? Well, in the company of an American Indian, he becomes an Indian himself. Alongside writer Eugene O'Neill, he starts to look like him although he doesn't grow the moustache. When he's with Jack Dempsey, he becomes a professional boxer, only he has glasses and a different physique. In the film, he also becomes a baseball player, a black jazz musician and a gangster!

Like many great comedies, *Zelig* is hilarious but it also makes some very serious points about identity and how we can become different people in different situations. For me, this makes it one of his best ever films, and it must certainly be his most original.

9.5 Speaking task, page 101, Exercise 5

Name: Melanie Fulton

Income per month	
'take home' pay	800
any other income	100
Total income	900
Expenses per month	
accommodation	250
transport	50
bills (telephone, gas, electricity)	125
subscriptions (magazines, TV, gym)	0
food	100
eating out and entertainment	250
clothes, shoes	200
Total expenses	....
Income minus expenses	....

Review C, Unit 8, page 103, Grammar, Exercise 3b

b) cans

Review D, Unit 10, page 136, Grammar, Exercise 1b

1 c) North America
2 b) England
3 c) 275 million people
4 b) English

1.1, *p. 4, Ex 3*

Ellen

Here in Wales there are two official languages – Welsh and English. Everybody speaks English, but not everybody speaks Welsh – but all road signs and official documents are in both languages. I have two first languages. I speak English and Welsh, and so do all my family. I usually speak Welsh at home, and I studied in both languages at school. I learned French at school as a foreign language, so I speak some French, but I never practise it, so I've forgotten a lot of it. Oh, I also speak a little Japanese – very little! I'm studying it at the moment.

Ernesto

Hi! I'm Ernesto. I'm from Paraguay. My first language is Guaraní – that's the language I learned first. My second language is Spanish. It isn't my mother tongue, but I learned it when I was very small! We have two languages in my country, because Guaraní and Spanish are both official languages in Paraguay. Most government forms and school books are in both languages. Most people here are bilingual, so they speak both languages really well!

1.9, *p. 13, Ex 5*

Sandra

This year, I don't have much time to study English, because of my job, but I plan to spend about four hours a week working on English. I like music and films, so I plan to listen to music and to watch films in English once or twice a week. You can learn a lot of vocabulary and slang from this, and it's fun. Sometimes in class I forget what I learned before, so I plan to read my notes before class to help me to remember what we talked about in the last class. I also plan to study my notes from class when I'm doing my homework. Homework usually takes me about two hours a week. I think this is all I'll have time for.

Max

This year, I think I can spend about eight hours a week studying English – one hour in the morning every day before work, and three hours at the weekend. I have homework twice a week, and I plan to spend a lot of time outside class studying vocabulary. I like to make lists of vocabulary and test myself – usually, I write the words by topic and then I write a translation next to the word. I plan to read whatever I can in English and write down all the new words in my vocabulary notebook. I'm an expert with my electronic dictionary – I'm very fast and I use it all the time to help me to understand new language when I'm reading magazines. I also plan to find exercises to help me practise online.

2.1, *p. 14, Ex 3*

Roxanne

I don't like cities, especially the one I live in. It's noisy and dirty! When I can, I like to go somewhere wild, in the middle of nature. My favourite place is the rainforest in the south of China. It's wet and rainy, but there's so much to see, you don't care! I took loads of photos of trees and animals. I didn't want to forget anything!

Juan

My favourite place in the world is a river in the north of Uruguay, not far from where I live. It's a really peaceful place, so quiet. I go to the river most weekends and fish... At least, I pretend to fish, but a lot of the time I just relax. OK, so if I'm honest, sometimes I fall asleep!

Sunee

I've lived on the island of Phuket in Thailand my whole life. It's small, but it's very friendly. My family and I often go to this beach on the east coast to meet friends and talk, and sometimes we eat here too. It's a lively place – there's always something happening.

Mohammed

I love walking, which is useful, I guess, because I work as a tour guide! The Moroccan desert can be dangerous, but it's very beautiful too, especially in the mountains in the west. I try to help visitors understand that this place is unique – there's nowhere quite like it.

2.5, *p. 18, Ex 3*

P = Presenter **S** = Steve

P: Welcome to Nature Watch. Our guest this morning is Steve Bolton, who won the World Wildlife Photographer competition a few days ago. Steve, it's a great photo. Was it difficult to take?

S: No, it was very easy! I took it last year, while my girlfriend and I were travelling through Bolivia. I was sitting next to a river and I saw the frog. It was jumping to catch an insect and luckily I had my camera with me... and that was it!

P: Being a photographer is an unusual job. How did it all start?

S: Oh, it started way back, when I was a kid. I got a camera for Christmas when I was eight – no, sorry, when I was seven. I absolutely loved it... When I was nine, I already knew I was going to be a photographer when I grew up. And here I am!

P: What are the best things about your job?

S: Well, I love travelling! I've been to Africa a lot, because my parents live in Nairobi, the capital of Kenya. But I didn't go there last year. For a change, I visited the south, from Australia to Antarctica – well, the northern part of Antarctica, anyway. Next year I'd like to go somewhere new, maybe North America, to photograph the bears. That'd be exciting!

P: Which animals do you like the best?

S: Butterflies and fish are pretty, but I really love working with big, wild animals, especially lions. I once took a great photo of one when I was working in Africa. It looked amazing while it was running – so beautiful. I don't like snakes, though. They're too dangerous!

P: I imagine working with animals can be difficult...

S: Well, they often surprise you! Once, while I was filming birds in the desert, a monkey ran away with my lunch! On another trip, a crocodile ate my bag – with my mobile inside!

P: How awful!

S: Yeah, it wasn't funny at the time...

2.7, *p. 20, Ex 1*

Jan

A: We had a really great time on holiday. I've got to tell you about the first night, because it was really funny. Something really strange happened...

B: Yeah, what?

A: Well, we spent ages shopping, so we were late getting to the campsite. While we were driving there it got really dark. So we put the tent up quickly, then we went to bed. Anyway, early in the morning, we heard this really strange noise... It woke everyone up, because it was so loud... And that's not all. It didn't sound, well, human...

B: Ooh, frightening!

A: Yeah, it was! Jacek and I wanted to call for help, but Agata told us not to be silly... While we were talking about what to do, she opened the tent door and you won't believe what happened...

B: What?

A: This, uh, cow, put its head right inside the tent! There were cows everywhere!... It seems we were camping in the wrong place!

B: That's crazy!

B: Yep, it was crazy alright, but really funny! We laughed for ages. I'll never forget it.

Lucia

A: It was a fantastic holiday – really great. Well... apart from the last day that is! We had a bit of a scary experience!

B: Oh no, what happened?

A: Well, we were driving through a safari park when some monkeys jumped onto the car! We were driving along, looking at all the animals. Some monkeys were following us when suddenly they jumped onto the roof. We could see them through the windows.

B: Oh no!

A: It was a bit scary! They were making a lot of noise! Then one of them climbed through

the window and took my sunglasses!
B: No! I don't believe it!
A: Yes! Then it ran away with them – and they were really expensive! Anyway, then some men came and chased the monkeys away.
B: That sounds... er, interesting, Lucia. The thing is, I've got to go, I've got some friends coming over and... Shall I call you later?

2.9, *p. 22, Ex 2*

Conversation 1
A: Good morning, can I have your passport, please?
B: Yes, Of course, here it is.
A: Where are you travelling to, sir?
B: Singapore...
A: Do you have your flight reference number with you?
B: Yes, here you are.
A: Thanks very much. How many bags do you want to check in?
B: Just this one...
A: Did you pack the bag yourself?
B: Yes.
A: You didn't leave it unattended at any time?
B: No, no.
A: Ok, thank you. Sir, I'm afraid there is a delay on your flight.
B: Oh dear... How long is it?
A: I'm not sure. They'll inform you at the boarding gate. Please go straight through to passport control now.
B: Oh, that's terrible, I'm going to miss my connection.
A: Here's a free pass to our business lounge, you'll be more comfortable there.
B: Oh, that's great... thank you!

Conversation 2
A: Hi, can I help?
B: Yes, can we check in, please. The name's Mantel.
A: Of course, do you have your booking reference number?
B: Yes, here it is, we booked online.
A: What was the name, again?
B: Mantel.
A: Ah yes, here you are, a double room arriving 15th and leaving on the 17th... Is that correct?
B: That's right. Just one question.
A: Certainly...
B: Is breakfast included?
A: Let me check, sir... Yes, that's right. Breakfast is from 7 to 10. And I have some good news for you, you have a suite!
B: Oh, that's a surprise. Thanks very much.
A: Here's your key... room 202... Leave your bags and we'll take them up to your room. Enjoy your stay!
B: Thanks, we will! One more thing...
A: Yes ?
B: Is there Wi-Fi in the rooms?
A: Yes, but there's an extra cost for internet. Here are the details.
B: Oh, that's a shame.

3.1, *p. 24, Ex 1*

A: So, do you remember The Seven Wonders of the Modern World, Jack?
B: Oh yes, wasn't it some kind of online competition or something?
A: Yes, that's it, quite a few years ago, now... 2007, I think. A Swiss-Canadian, Bernard Weber, set up the project. He asked people to vote on the seven best constructions in the world today, is that right?
B: Yes, I remember – first people from around the world nominated their favourite landmarks – they all had to be man-made – and then everyone voted for the top seven. The winners were announced on July the 7th 2007, the seventh of the seventh of 2007!
A: I don't think I can name all seven though!
B: Well, in alphabetical order they are: Chichen Itza – the Mayan pyramid in the Yucatan Peninsula, Mexico...
A: Oh, yes. I've been there – it's wonderful.
B: The Christ the Redeemer statue in Rio de Janeiro, Brazil...
A: Oh yes, there's a great view of the city from there. I've never been, but I've seen photos. Amazing!
B: The Colosseum in Rome...
A: Of course!
B: The 6,000 kilometre-long Great Wall of China...
A: I'd love to go to China to see that – they say it's the only man-made structure that you can see from space.
B: The Inca city of Machu Picchu, near Cuzco in Peru...
A: Another place I've always wanted to visit.
B: Petra, the city made in rock, in Jordan...
A: Oh yes, that really is such a beautiful place.
B: ... and the Taj Mahal in Agra, India.
A: I have been there. What a great list! But no pyramids? I mean the pyramids in Egypt?
B: No, they were on the original list – the Seven Wonders of the Ancient World...

3.10, *p. 32, Ex 2*

S = Sal J = Jake C = Carly D = Dave
S: OK. So what do you think? Which is your favourite, Jake?
J: Well, personally, I prefer the ones that show beautiful scenery, because I really like nature. What do you think, Carly?
C: But that's so boring. I'd rather have something modern. I like this design – it's really abstract and cool.
D: The problem is, you have to change your skin every two weeks if you like things that are in fashion! I'd prefer something more classic, like a piece of art. What about you, Sal? Which do you prefer?
S: I like that one. I'd like to have one that shows one of my hobbies or interests. I'd much rather have one that says something about me and who I am.
J: Well, really, if you want your laptop skin to say something about you, wouldn't it be better to have a custom design – something that you design yourself?
S: I suppose you're right. Or... what about no design at all? What if you don't want people to know anything about you? Which is better?
D: I hadn't really thought about that.

4.1, *p. 38, Ex 2*

1
Wow, I look so young in this photo... Many girls in Colombia have what's called a Quinceañera party when they're fifteen. All your friends and family are there. It's a great party. We all dress up in these lovely dresses – it's definitely much more important than a normal birthday party. It's when you become an adult. I remember we danced all night... I met my first boyfriend there! Did I feel like an adult afterwards? Not really. I was still at school. I couldn't drive a car. I didn't leave home till I was 25! But I had lots of fun and lots of presents!
2
We were both 28 when we got married. We were so nervous – and so happy. It really was a very special day. All our friends and family were there. Even my boss came! I don't think I stopped smiling all day! Did it make a difference? Well, yes, it did. I was surprised how big a difference it made. Some people say weddings are just an excuse for a party, but no, it's much, much more. When I look at the ring and think of that day, I know it changed my life for me.
3
This was such a wonderful day. And she's such an incredible lady. It was really hard to believe that she was 100 years old. She spoke so clearly and intelligently. Everybody was there to celebrate with her: her colleagues, her friends, her family. It really was a very special occasion.

4.7, *p. 46, Ex 2*

Photo A
A: Claudio!
B: Helen! Welcome back! Here, these are for you.
A: They're beautiful, thank you.
B: It's great to see you. I know it was just a week, but I've missed you, Helen.
A: Oh, me too... I mean, I've missed you, too. It was a really boring business trip, and I'm glad to be back! So tell me, how are things?
B: Oh, pretty good, yeah. It was fairly quiet at work this week so...

Photo B
A: George! It's great to see you again. It's been a long time since we last met. It must be what, twenty years now?
B: Twenty-two, I think..., yes, twenty-two since we retired from the school. It's good

to catch up, after all this time. It's a shame we've only got a few hours.

A: Yes, we must meet up again soon. So, what are you doing now?

B: Oh, I moved to Scotland when I stopped teaching... Did I tell you that my eldest son has a business in Edinburgh?

A: Yes, I remember... I'm glad he's been so successful.

B: Yes, we're very proud. How are your sons?

A: They're fine, thanks. They'd love to meet you...

Photo C

A: Oh, it's so good... it's so good to see you. Eight months. It's... it's been so long since I saw you.

B: Yeah, it is, it is... it's great to be back home again. So, Mum... how's it going?

A: Oh, not bad... we've been OK. But you don't want to hear about that! We all want to hear about you!

B: Well, I've got lots to tell you. Is Dad here? And everyone else?

A: Yes, they're all inside. They can't wait to see you.

5.1, *p. 49, Ex 2*

1
My candidate for the Teacher of the Year award is Professor Quarashi. Professor Quarashi teaches university courses in IT, or Information Technology. That's really unusual – not many women teach IT in Saudi Arabia. My family didn't want me to go to university. They wanted me to get married. But Professor Quarashi helped me. She spoke to my parents, and now I'm studying IT too. Professor Quarashi says it's important to choose your favourite subject for your degree, and I love computers! Thank you, Professor – you're my hero!

2
My vote goes to Matthew Sanford! Matthew teaches in the USA. He's disabled and he needs to use a wheelchair. But he doesn't stay at home all day. He teaches yoga! He believes everyone can do something amazing – whoever you are and whatever problems you have. His yoga lessons are great, I really look forward to them. They're certainly much more fun than staying home and watching TV!

3
A & B: Vote for Phil!

A: Phil Higgins is our Science teacher. He teaches us at primary school.

B: Primary school is usually boring, but Mr Higgins makes it fun.

A: Yeah. And he's amazing because he's not just a Science teacher – he's a pilot too!

B: Yeah. Sophie and I, we go to a tiny school in Australia, miles from any towns. We've only got one classroom, and one teacher, Mrs Green. Mrs Green is a great teacher, but she doesn't teach Science. Mr Higgins is our Science teacher. And he's the best!

A: We love learning about science. Mr Higgins' Science lessons are great.

B: Yes, he flies his plane to our village once a week, and he teaches us Science outdoors. He thinks classrooms are ugly places!

A: And we think he should get the Teacher of the Year award.

5.3, *p. 50, Ex 1*

1 **Ilaria**

Hi, I'm Ilaria. I'm not doing anything exciting this summer, because I need to study. I'm taking my final exam in Forensic Science next month. Forensic Science is really popular now. I chose this course because I love TV police dramas like CSI and Bones, and I want to help the police find criminals. The problem is, thousands of students have had the same idea! I'm working really hard for this exam because I need to get a good grade.

2 **Raushan**

I'm Raushan. Next month, I'm going to start a degree in equine studies. In my home country, Kazakhstan, horses are very important: my family has several horses and we ride them in competitions. There aren't any Equine Studies degrees at my local university, so my family... we're moving to the USA in the new year and I'm going to study there. There are loads of equine courses in the USA – you can even take a course in horse psychology, so you can learn how horses think! But I'm more interested in learning about health and medicine. I want to help our horses be strong, fit – and win lots of prizes!

3 **Lee**

Hi, I'm Lee. At first, I wanted to study Sports Science at uni, 'cause I love football. But I couldn't make my mind up. I didn't know if I'd enjoy studying sport instead of playing it. Then I heard about this new course at Birmingham University, all about social networking – chatting to friends online, that sort of thing. I already spend half my time doing that! I'm starting the course next year, and I'm getting excited about it already. My parents don't think it's a 'real' degree – they want me to study a traditional subject, like, I dunno, Chemistry. But I think the internet – that's the future, isn't it? It might be 'trendy' now, but in ten years' time it's going to be like history or literature – everybody's going to be doing it!

5.9, *p. 56, Intonation*

1 **A:** Please can I sit here?
B: Please can I sit here?

2 **A:** Could you help me, please?
B: Could you help me, please?

3 **A:** Would you like to come?
B: Would you like to come?

5.10, *p. 57, Ex 2*

A: Hello. Adventures in English here. How can I help you?

B: Er, good morning! I read an advertisement about your school in the *International Times*, and it sounds very interesting. Could I ask you a few more questions?

A: Certainly. What would you like to know?

B: Well, first of all could you tell me where your students stay?

A: Sure. Students stay in a big hotel near the famous Sydney Bridge. Lots of our students like to take photos there!

B: That sounds nice... I'd like to know more about the courses. What subjects do you teach?

A: Well, there's English, of course! But you can also choose extra classes in Literature, Art and Music. Music is always very popular!

B: OK, thanks... I'd also like to know how big your classes are.

A: They're quite small. We usually have between five and ten students in a class. No more than that.

B: Great, thanks. Sorry, I have another question. What activities can students do after school?

A: Oh, there's lots! Students can do sports, walk around the city, or they can go to the cinema. We also take students on trips to the coast.

B: One last question... What does your course cost?

A: It's $600 a week!

B: $600! But the plane ticket's $550! Oh dear, I need to think about this... Could I call you later?

A: Of course, whenever you like.

B: Thank you. Thanks for your help.

6.1, *p. 58, Ex 2*

1
This is a great story. It's about how teenagers are volunteering to help older people learn how to use computers. They don't just help them with technical things. They teach them about fun things too – finding clips from their favourite films, or their favourite singers, scanning and copying old photos, helping them find the news they're interested in... and it's not only about computers. It's about building bridges in the community, bringing the old and the young together, helping them understand each other's worlds. There should be more projects like this.

2
I know this sounds like a joke – but it really did happen. I was there. I saw it. There was a cat stuck in the tree, and its owner called the firefighters – they had to use their ladder and everything. It was very difficult, but in the end they got the cat down. I don't think it was the best possible use of the emergency services! But I suppose it gave them some extra practice for when there's a real emergency!

3
We help out at a local charity – I go out

every Sunday if I can – and we were out one day, handing out food and talking to the homeless people down by the market. It was cold, and we were giving them soup and bread. Anyway, we were there as usual, and this young kid walked over, he was just a passerby, and he walked up to one man and offered him his burger – the burger his dad had just bought for him. His dad was nodding and smiling, and the homeless man smiled too – it was such a nice, generous gesture.

6.2, *p. 61, Ex 2*

N = Natalie J = Jason

J: Umm Natalie, can I take this afternoon off as holiday?

N: Hmm, I don't know Jason. You should finish that report for the presentation tomorrow.

J: I know, but I can't do any more today. I'm still waiting for the information I need from John Bodley.

N: Well, you should call him and tell him you need it urgently.

J: I know, I've called a few times and left a message. He hasn't called back yet. The thing is… I'm going to play football, to make some money for the local hospital. I can't say no, can I?

N: Well, I suppose it's OK this time. But you shouldn't ask for time off on the same day – you should ask at least a week before.

J: Sorry, Natalie. Thanks. I can finish the report this evening.

6.10, *p. 66, Ex 2*

1 A: I'm not feeling well. I have a headache and a fever.
B: Why don't you go home and go to bed?

2 A: There's a fire in the kitchen!
B: You should call the emergency number.

3 A: I'm not doing well in college, because I miss you so much. What should I do?
B: You should ask someone for help. Why don't you speak to your teacher and see what she says?

4 A: I've got terrible problems at work. I'm so stressed. Do you think I should talk to my boss?
B: There are people who can help with stress. Why don't you talk to a professional?

5 A: I'm going to be late for class. What can I do?
B: What about calling your friend? She can let someone know.

6 A: Oh no! This woman has fainted!
B: Quick, you need to call a doctor.

[illegible]

P = Presenter J = Jan T = Tanya

P: On today's programme, we're visiting two unusual restaurants. The first one is called the Restaurant of the Future, and it's at Wageningen University in the Netherlands. We spoke to science correspondent Jan Walters to learn why it's so unusual. … Hi, Jan. Well, it doesn't look like a futuristic restaurant. So, what's so special about this place?

J: Well, it looks like a normal university canteen – and in fact it is a normal university canteen. The interesting thing is that it's also a laboratory.

P: What do you mean, a laboratory?

J: Well, there are ten cameras in the canteen, which film people as they eat and drink. Here on these screens, the researchers watch how people make a choice about what to eat and drink. Scientists are studying the science of food, doing research into why people eat and drink the way they do. And they're getting a lot of very interesting data. More than 250 students at the university are taking part in the project. Of course, the students don't know what the scientists are looking for, but they do their best to co-operate. The scientists have already made progress, in fact they've made some surprising discoveries.

P: For example…?

J: Well, they've discovered that, on average, women spend longer deciding what to eat than men. And they make changes – very small changes – in the lighting, the decoration, etc. and they've noticed, for example, that people eat more food when there are flowers on their table.

P: That's interesting… And what kind of food do people eat?

J: Oh, all sorts! Manufacturers often ask the researchers to do work on new food in the restaurant, so the menu is always changing. They also do tests on all kinds of things: how much food people leave on their plate, how quickly they make a decision about what to eat… lots of things…

P: Now, our second destination is a very different kind of restaurant of the future. We're in London's Soho, in an oriental fusion restaurant called Inamo. I spoke to restaurant critic, Tanya Ballesta. … Hi Tanya.

T: Hi there. How are you?

P: So, tell us, how is this the restaurant of the future, then?

T: Well, the first thing to notice is the lighting and the decoration. The interior designers did lots of different experiments before they chose this. They have created a special atmosphere, like a science-fiction movie. I think it's great!

P: And they've invented a new system for ordering food, is that right?

T: Yes, as you can see, the tables are touch-sensitive and interactive. Each table has a projector and a track pad, so you can see the food flash up on the table top in front of you.Then while you are waiting, you can watch the chef making food on a live web cam, and even play a video game on your table.

P: So, there are no people serving?

T: There's no one taking your order, but the waiter brings the food to your table. That way it's much quicker, and there are no mistakes! And when you've finished, you can order a taxi to take you home by simply clicking a button.

P: It all seems a bit too high tech for me.

T: Well, they're experimenting with new ideas all the time, and most people love the novelty value. One day all restaurants might be like this!

[illegible]

1 **Fontez**

How much technology do I use? Not much! I want to help the environment, so I try not to use lots of energy. It helps me to save a little money too, which is great. I hate shopping, it's so boring! I don't have a lot of things. I don't have a TV, an MP3 player, or even a fridge, nothing like that. Do I ever miss technology? Um, if I'm honest, yes, I do, sometimes. A computer would be great – I love surfing the net, there's a lot of fascinating information out there. At first I didn't use to have any gadgets or electric items at all, but a few years ago I bought myself a small electric fire. Where I live, it can get cold in winter – really cold! But I try not to use it for too many hours a day.

2 **Bella**

When I use technology, I feel really ill. I get a terrible headache, and then I have to go to bed. It isn't much fun! My doctor told me that technology can make a few people feel sick. This is a huge problem for me! Just look around you the next time you're in town: how many gadgets do you see? Nearly everyone seems to have mobile phones, MP3 players … there aren't many places I can visit without getting a headache, so I usually stay in! I think, some day, I'll have to move. There are still lots of countries where people don't use much technology, like parts of Africa. I'd like to go there – it would be good to feel well again.

3 **Kerim**

I live in a place which doesn't have any electricity, so there isn't much technology. I don't care – it isn't a problem for me. I don't need a lot of gadgets to be happy – I think people spend too much time watching TV and playing computer games anyway. I'd rather spend more time having fun with my friends and family! I'm not really interested in science and technology, and I get bored when we have to study it at school. I'm much more interested in music. I want to be a musician when I leave school, like my dad. I'd like to be like him.

INFINITIVE	PAST SIMPLE	PAST PARTICIPLE
be	was, were	been
become	became	become
begin	began	begun
bite	bit	bitten
break	broke	broken
bring	brought	brought
build	built	built
buy	bought	bought
choose	chose	chosen
come	came	come
cost	cost	cost
do	did	done
dream	dreamt/dreamed	dreamt/dreamed
drink	drank	drunk
eat	ate	eaten
fall	fell	fallen
feel	felt	felt
find	found	found
fly	flew	flown
forbid	forbade	forbidden
forget	forgot	forgotten
forgive	forgave	forgiven
get	got	got
give	gave	given
go	went	gone, been
grow	grew	grown
have	had	had
hear	heard	heard
hide	hid	hidden
hold	held	held
keep	kept	kept
know	knew	known
learn	learnt/learned	learnt/learned
leave	left	left
let	let	let
lose	lost	lost
make	made	made
meet	met	met
pay	paid	paid
put	put	put
read /ri:d/	read /red/	read /red/
ride	rode	ridden
ring	rang	rung
rise	rose	risen
run	ran	run
say	said	said
see	saw	seen
sell	sold	sold
send	sent	sent
set	set	set
shake	shook	shaken
show	showed	shown
shut	shut	shut
sing	sang	sung
sit	sat	sat
sleep	slept	slept
speak	spoke	spoken
spend	spent	spent
stand	stood	stood
steal	stole	stolen
stick	stuck	stuck
swim	swam	swum
take	took	taken
teach	taught	taught
tell	told	told
think	thought	thought
throw	threw	thrown
understand	understood	understood
wake	woke	woken
wear	wore	worn
win	won	won
write	wrote	written

CONTENTS

The BIG Picture

PRE-INTERMEDIATE A

Workbook

ALASTAIR LANE

Richmond

1 SPEAKING THE SAME LANGUAGE

VOCABULARY

Languages

1 Find ten countries in the word search.

X	V	K	W	Q	F	Y	H	P	E	R	U
B	R	A	Z	I	L	V	B	J	S	R	V
R	G	M	Z	Y	K	U	E	W	R	Z	M
U	I	N	D	I	A	Q	L	L	X	J	W
J	R	V	L	Z	P	W	G	P	F	A	B
A	U	S	T	R	A	L	I	A	H	P	X
F	E	Z	F	J	C	V	U	Z	P	A	K
K	G	X	H	J	S	M	M	Y	V	N	C
Z	Y	Y	Q	U	R	X	Q	L	X	K	H
J	P	G	H	O	L	L	A	N	D	Y	I
S	T	H	W	C	M	Q	B	C	F	J	N
R	V	W	G	K	E	N	Y	A	C	S	A

2 Complete the sentences with the words from the box.

Arabic Cantonese Dutch English French Hindi Japanese Mandarin Portuguese Spanish Swahili

1 People talk about 'Chinese', but actually this is two languages: ___________ and ___________ .
2 ___________ is the language of the Netherlands, not German!
3 ___________ is the international language of business, computing and the internet.
4 In Lisbon and Rio de Janeiro, the official language is ___________ .
5 People in most Middle Eastern countries speak ___________ .
6 ___________ is an African language. It's an official language in Kenya, Tanzania and Uganda.
7 In Tokyo and Osaka, people speak ___________ .
8 ___________ is the second language of Canada. People speak it as a first language in Quebec.
9 People speak ___________ in almost every country in Latin America.
10 ___________ is an Indian language, and many people speak it there.

3 Complete the text with language words.

My name is Tove, and I come from Turku in Finland. There are two (1) o _ f _ c _ _ _ languages in my country: Finnish and Swedish. In fact, my home town has another name: in Swedish it's called Åbo. So, a lot of people are (2) b _ l _ _ g _ _ _ here, including me. I have two (3) f _ _ _ t languages because I grew up with Swedish and Finnish. But really my (4) m _ _ h _ r tongue is Swedish because I speak that at home with my parents. At school I also learnt some (5) f _ r _ _ _ _ languages like French and German, but my main (6) s _ c _ _ d language is English. Most people in the Nordic countries speak it really well!

Free time

4 Look at the pictures. Complete the sentences.

1 I like going out but I prefer h___________ friends r___________ .

2 My brother spends hours s___________ the i___________ .

3 If you like dancing, come out with us – we love g___________ c___________ .

4 Dad's r___________ the n___________ in the living room.

5 My parents love e___________ o___________ at restaurants.

6 Tim wants to be a model so he's g___________ to the g___________ a lot at the moment.

Communication

5 Correct the wrong sentences. Tick (✓) two correct sentences.

1 The doctor wants to tell you something.
____

2 The teacher says us the answers at the end of the class.
____

3 My mother talks her sister on the phone every day.
____

4 Listen to your boss! He gives you good advice.
____

5 Jon loves talking to computers with his friends.
____

6 All politicians say lies.
____

7 Do you listen that strange noise? What is it?
____

8 My brother and I receive emails to each other all the time.
____

VOCABULARY EXTENSION
Other free time words

6 Replace the words in **bold** with words from the pictures.

stamps

fishing

piano

a blog

roller-blading

horse

1 My brother loves riding his **motorbike** at the weekend. *horse*
2 In my free time, I usually play the **guitar**. _______
3 My dad's hobby is collecting **CDs**. _______
4 They live near the beach so they often go **swimming** in the sea. _______
5 When I want to do some exercise, I usually go **cycling**. _______
6 Jim writes **songs** in his free time. _______

BRING IT TOGETHER

7 **a** Complete the conversations with the words from the box. There is one word that you don't need in each conversation.

Conversation A

Arabic	bilingual	play
round	talk	tell	writes

A I've got an email from Hernan. He isn't coming to the football game today.

B What? But we always (1) _______ football on Saturdays.

A It's not his fault. His parents are having some old friends (2) _______. One of them is a journalist in Egypt. She's (3) _______ – she speaks English and (4) _______. Hernan wants to (5) _______ to her about her job.

B Does he want to be a journalist then?

A Yeah! That's his dream job. He (6) _______ a blog for the university magazine already.

Conversation B

hearing listening reading
roller-blading sending
surfing talking

C Mum!

D What is it, Jackie? I'm busy. I'm (1) _______ the newspaper.

C I'm bored. I want to go (2) _______ in the park, but it's raining.

D Well, there are lots of things to do indoors.

C Like what?

D Well, your brother's (3) _______ the internet. Why don't you do that with him?

C No, I don't want to. He's only (4) _______ emails. He isn't doing anything fun.

D Well, what about (5) _______ to music?

C No. I want to phone my friend Tina, but Dad's (6) _______ to someone on the phone.

b 1.1 Listen and check.

GRAMMAR
Present simple & present continuous

1 Choose the correct sentence ending, a or b.

1 Frank doesn't drive
  a because he doesn't have a driving licence.
  b because there's a problem with his car today.
2 Every time we go to Paris
  a we stay at the same hotel.
  b we're staying at the same hotel.
3 We've just bought a new house so
  a we buy a lot of new furniture.
  b we're buying a lot of new furniture at the moment.
4 What's that noise?
  a Does your mobile ring?
  b Is your mobile ringing?
5 There are two official languages in Finland –
  a people speak Finnish and Swedish.
  b people are speaking Finnish and Swedish.
6 Dagmar loves pets –
  a she has three cats and a dog!
  b she's having three cats and a dog!

2 Complete the sentences about the pictures using the verbs in **bold**.

1 **play**
  a Mike __________________ football every weekend.
  b Mike __________________ football at the moment.

2 **buy**
  a Jacques and Carmen __________________ lots of books.
  b Jacques and Carmen __________________ some books.

3 **take**
  a We __________________ the dog for a walk.
  b We usually __________________ the dog for a walk in the morning.

4 **teach**
  a I __________________ my son to ride a bike.
  b I __________________ Maths at the local school.

3 Write sentences about what you are doing now.

1 I *'m not cooking* dinner.
2 I __________________ the guitar.
3 I __________________ an exercise in my English book.
4 I __________________ on the phone to my friends.
5 I __________________ a bike.
6 I __________________ on a chair.

Questions

4 Put the words in the correct order to make questions.

1 from where come your teacher does

______

2 you out like do eating

______

3 film your is favourite what

______

4 do round how they friends have often

______

5 you are why late

______

6 students how class the many in are

______

5 Correct one mistake in each conversation.

1 A What means 'ride'?
  B It means 'to travel', for example on a bike or a horse.

2 A How often go you to the gym?
  B We go there every day.

3 A Do Mineko and Toshi work in the restaurant?
  B No, they not.

4 A When does our class starts?
  B It starts at 5 p.m.

5 A Are Becky and Laura come from England?
  B No, they're Irish.

6 A Do you like cooking?
  B Yes, I like.

Bring it together

6 Choose the correct option to complete the web chat.

tihana Louise! Hello from Croatia!

louise Hi, Tihana!

tihana Why (1) *are you surfing / do you surf* the internet now? What time (2) *it is / is it* in Australia?

louise It's 2 a.m. over here! But don't worry, this is normal for me – (3) *I'm working / I work* at this time every day.

tihana Why?

louise (4) *I'm having / I have* a new job. I'm an astronomer on a project here in Australia. I study the sky at night.

tihana An astronomer? Wow! (5) *What / When* are you studying at the moment?

louise Asteroids.

tihana Asteroids! How (6) *are people researching / do people research* asteroids?

louise (7) *We're usually looking / We usually look* at them with telescopes and then (8) *we're studying / we study* the results on the computer. That's what (9) *I do / I'm doing* at the moment.

tihana So are any asteroids travelling towards Earth right now?

louise Ha ha! (10) *You're watching / You watch* too many movies. Don't worry – you're safe!

FUNCTIONAL LANGUAGE Checking understanding

1 Complete the sentences and questions with verbs from the box. There is one verb that you don't need.

call hear listen mean say speak

1 What do you ___________ this kind of book in English?
2 Could you ___________ more slowly, please?
3 I'm sorry, I didn't ___________ you.
4 What does 'bilingual' ___________ ?
5 Can you ___________ that number again, please?

2 Match 1–5 in **1** to responses a–e.

a Sorry, was I speaking too quickly? Is this better? ____
b 'Speaking two languages equally well.' ____
c It's so noisy... I asked you what you liked doing in your free time. ____
d Sure. 6-8-7-6-0-7. That's 6-8-7-6-0-7. ____
e It's a 'dictionary'. ____

LISTENING Preparing to listen

1 You are going to listen to three conversations. Before you listen, read the web post and profiles quickly. Who are Sara, Keito and Roos?

a Tourists visiting an information office. ____
b Information officers who work in New York. ____
c People who want to work in an information office. ____

STRATEGY Look at any photos, tables or texts before you listen. They can give you clues about what you're going to hear.

FRIENDLY, SOCIABLE PEOPLE WANTED!
Do you enjoy going out in the city – and telling people about your favourite places? Are you good at languages? Our New York tourist information office needs a summer assistant. Click **here** for details.

Candidate 1: Sara
Languages: (1) ___________
Interests: (2) ___________

Candidate 2: Keito
Languages: (3) ___________
Interests: (4) ___________

Candidate 3: Roos
Languages: (5) ___________
Interests: (6) ___________

2 **a** Look at the profiles again. Choose four words or expressions which you might need to complete them.

Australian doing homework English going clubbing
Holland surfing the internet Spanish working

b 1.2 Listen and check.

3 Listen again and complete the profiles in **1**. Who do you think is best for the job?

STRATEGY Always read the task carefully and make sure you understand what you need to do. Don't try to read the task for the first time while you listen, or you might miss important information.

READING Skimming

1 Read the webpage quickly and choose the best description.

a a homepage for a language camp ____
b an article about language camps ____
c a factual report on a language camp ____
d a review of a language camp ____

STRATEGY Read the whole text quickly before you answer any questions. What type of text is it (a letter, an article, a report...)? What is it mainly about?

One World Camp

(1) ____________

This August, spend a holiday at our award-winning One World Camp in the beautiful Canadian mountains. Every year, we help hundreds of students to learn new language skills – and make new friends!

(2) ____________

Our classes are suitable for students aged 14–16, for older students/adults, and for families. All nationalities are welcome – we teach students from all over the world.

(3) ____________

Right now, we're offering programmes in English, Spanish, French, Italian, Portuguese, German, Mandarin and Arabic, and we're planning to offer Japanese classes next year. Some of our teachers also speak Cantonese and Hindi, although we don't teach these languages in our official programme.

(4) ____________

Students have lots of time for fun, too, with two free days a week, and a big choice of activities. Many people enjoy playing music, painting and playing sport. Or why not be adventurous and try canoeing or paragliding? We don't have any Wi-Fi at the camp, but students say they never feel bored here!

(5) ____________

Still thinking? Then read these comments from last year's students.

The teachers are friendly and experienced, and the courses are excellent. Amazingly, the camp isn't very expensive! ☆☆☆☆☆ **Sanjit, USA, 45**

One World is lots of fun. But there are too many great activities to try! I want to stay longer. :) ☆☆☆☆ **Kasia, Poland, 18**

(6) ____________

We'd love to hear from you! Fill in our online form for more information.

Identifying key ideas

2 Read the webpage again and choose headings for paragraphs 1–6. There are two headings that you don't need.

a **Reviews** ____
b **Our courses** ____
c **Prices** ____
d **Free time** ____
e **Accommodation** ____
f **Our students** ____
g **About us** ____
h **Find out more** ____

STRATEGY In a text there is usually a different paragraph for each main idea. Read the text carefully and try to decide what the most important ideas are in each paragraph.

2 BACK TO NATURE

VOCABULARY

Geography

1 Complete the words.

1 In Morocco, we rode camels in the d __ s __ r __ . It was really hot and dry there, but it was cool when we went high up in the Atlas M __ __ nt __ __ __ s.
2 Last year we stayed in a hotel in Croatia on the c __ a __ t. It was really near the s __ __ , and we spent all day on the b __ a __ __ .
3 I was born on an i __ l __ __ __ in the Pacific Ocean that's far from e __ __ r __ w __ __ r __ .
4 My grandparents live in a house in the c __ __ __ __ __ y. It's on the b __ __ __ s of a river.
5 We went camping in a f __ __ e __ __ last summer. It was nice to walk through the trees.

2 Look at the map of Peru. Correct the wrong information. Tick (✓) two correct sentences.

1 Cusco is inland.
____
2 Lima is on an island.
____
3 Trujillo is on the east coast of Peru.
____
4 Arequipa is in the east of Peru.
____
5 Huánuco is in the centre of Peru.
____
6 Iquitos is near the capital, Lima.
____

3 Complete the email with words from the box.

beach centre coast
forest island near

Hello from the island of Bali! We're having a fantastic time here. At the moment, we're staying near Ubud, in the (1) ____________ of the (2) ____________ . Our hotel is in a (3) ____________ – we can hear monkeys in the trees around us! Next we plan to go to Kuta. It's on the (4) ____________ , quite (5) ____________ the capital, Denpasar. We want to spend a few days relaxing on the (6) ____________ before we come home!

Love,

Miranda

Animals

4 a Find ten animal words in the word search.

V	M	D	R	Z	Y	L	H	Z	Q
D	C	A	T	J	B	I	M	R	G
Q	V	K	C	R	B	O	K	V	I
P	P	C	H	A	B	N	F	Y	R
I	Q	O	S	B	K	Q	X	D	A
G	C	W	F	B	M	U	H	P	F
R	Z	B	P	I	J	F	O	X	F
K	J	X	G	T	C	H	U	C	E
D	E	E	R	Y	V	V	D	R	J
M	B	X	S	H	E	E	P	S	G
S	M	O	N	K	E	Y	G	M	Z

b Circle the option that doesn't work.

1 You get milk from *cows* / *foxes* / *sheep*.
2 A *giraffe* / *polar bear* / *sheep* is white.
3 My brother has a pet *cat* / *rabbit* / *lion*.
4 *Horses* / *Monkeys* / *Snakes* climb trees.
5 A male *deer* / *dog* / *lion* has a different head from the female.

Vocabulary extension
Other animal words

5 a Look at the pictures. Complete the sentences.

1 *Lizards* are reptiles. You often see them running up the walls of houses in hot countries.
2 The __________ is a type of insect. They live inside homes, and in dirty places.
3 __________ produce milk, like sheep and cows.
4 __________ are grey birds that live in cities. They often eat food dropped by tourists.
5 The blue __________ is the largest animal in the sea.
6 __________, for example, tarantulas, are not insects because they have eight legs.
7 The __________ is a very common pet in many countries.
8 The __________ is a very large bird. It is the national symbol of Mexico, Russia and the USA.

b 2.1 Listen and check.

Bring it together

6 Complete the web posts with the words from the box. There is one word that you don't need.

beach capital coast eagle fox
mountains sea south whales

ANIMALS Search:

Post: Messages • Status • Photos • Videos •

Welcome to the website of The Wild Beast show. We want to know about your amazing animal experiences. Post your messages below!

Zvonimir
Hi, Wild Beast Show! I'm from Croatia, but I have a story from your country. Last year, I was in a park in London with some friends when we saw a (1) __________ . It was chasing a rabbit, but it didn't catch it. Amazing! Imagine that – two wild animals in the middle of Britain's (2) __________ city!

Erica
I have a story from my country. When I was a child my parents took me to Guerrero Negro on the west (3) __________ of Mexico. We went in a boat and we saw lots of (4) __________ ! They were swimming in the (5) __________ next to our boat. It was a great experience – they're really beautiful animals.

Kurt
Last winter, I was hiking in the (6) __________ with my friends. We were in the Pyrénées, in the (7) __________ of France. On the first day, after four hours, we sat down to have a break and a drink. Suddenly, we saw an (8) __________ right next to us. It was a really beautiful bird. We watched it for ages – it was an incredible moment!

GRAMMAR

Past simple

1 Complete the table with the past simple form of the verbs from the box.

~~climb~~	eat	find	fly	go	leave
need	make	sleep	stay	walk	

Regular verbs	Irregular verbs
climbed	

2 Complete the interview with the past simple form of the verbs in brackets.

A life in 6 questions...

Magda Laws (35), a naturalist in Uganda

Q1 **Magda, how (1) ____________ *(you/become)* a naturalist?**

A I (2) ____________ *(be born)* on a farm in Zimbabwe. There were always animals around the house, and I was fascinated by them.

Q2 **Why (3) ____________ *(you/decide)* to work with chimpanzees?**

A I got the idea when I (4) ____________ *(read)* about the work of Jane Goodall. She worked with chimpanzees in Tanzania and she really (5) ____________ *(change)* people's ideas about them.

Q3 **(6) ____________ *(you/study)* Zoology at university?**

A Actually, I (7) ____________ *(not/go)* to university. I (8) ____________ *(not/want)* to spend years reading books. I came directly to Uganda.

Q4 **Was life difficult in the beginning?**

A No, never. I love Uganda. I (9) ____________ *(not/think)* about going anywhere else.

Q5 **What was your best experience here?**

A On my first morning, I got up very early and I (10) ____________ *(walk)* through the jungle. I was 19, and my life suddenly felt like one big adventure.

Q6 **Do you have any advice for people who want to do the same as you?**

A When I decided to come here, lots of people (11) ____________ *(tell)* me it was a bad idea. I (12) ____________ *(not/listen)* to them. That's my advice. Trust yourself!

Past continuous

3 Write past continuous sentences for pictures 1–6.

When they heard the news...

1 Judith ____________________________ . *(shop/in the supermarket)*
2 Diego and Jim ____________________________ . *(have/a coffee)*
3 Brendan ____________________________ . *(relax/at home)*
4 Piotr ____________________________ . *(cook/dinner)*
5 Lisa ____________________________ . *(drive/home)*
6 Karen and Irma ____________________________ . *(surf/the internet)*

Past simple & past continuous

4 Change one verb in each sentence to the past continuous.

1 Hiro broke his arm while he ~~skied~~.
was skiing
2 When I met Jason, I worked in a burger bar.
____
3 The phone rang four times while we had dinner.
____
4 It didn't rain when I left the house.
____
5 I saw your mum while I walked the dog.
____
6 When Emanuelle lived in the USA, she went to New York and LA.
____
7 While I walked to work, Mehmet called me.
____
8 I bought a newspaper while I waited at the station.
____

BRING IT TOGETHER

5 Choose the correct options to complete the news story.

The Tasmanian Tiger

One day in 1995, Australian Charlie Beasley (1) *looked / was looking* for birds in Tasmania when he (2) *saw / was seeing* something incredible – an animal that looked like a dog but with tiger stripes, and a tail like a kangaroo. Beasley was sure that it was a thylacine – the famous Tasmanian Tiger! Most scientists believe that the last one (3) *died / was dying* in 1936. But could thylacines still be alive? It was impossible to say, because Beasley (4) *didn't take / wasn't taking* a photo. However, in 2005, two German tourists (5) *travelled / were travelling* through Tasmania when they too (6) *found / were finding* a thylacine. They (7) *discovered / were discovering* the animal when they (8) *got / were getting* water. Amazingly, they (9) *took / were taking* some photos too! But when Australian newspapers asked to see the photos, they (10) *decided / were deciding* not to buy them because they weren't sure if the pictures were real. So still today, the world is waiting to see if the thylacine is still alive, hiding somewhere in the jungles of Tasmania.

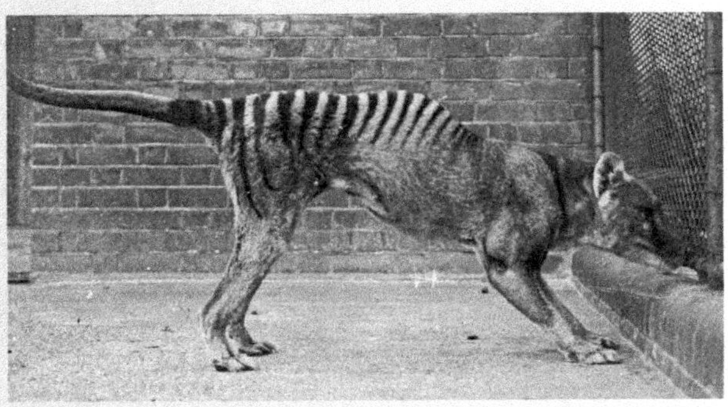

FUNCTIONAL LANGUAGE

Checking in

1 Read conversations 1–7 and write *airport* (A), *hotel* (H) or *both* (B).

	Location	Conversation
1	H	A I'm pleased to tell you, you have a suite! B Oh, that's great. Thank you!
2	____	A How many bags do you want to check in? B ________ this one.
3	____	A Can I have your tickets and passports, please? B Yes, of ________. Here they are.
4	____	A Here's a free pass to the gym and pool. B Oh, that's a ________. Thanks very much!
5	____	A Do you have your booking reference number? B Yes, ________ it is. We booked online.
6	____	A I'm afraid there's an extra cost for breakfast. B Oh, that's a ________.
7	____	A I'm afraid there's a delay to your flight. B Oh, ________. How long is it?

2 Complete the conversations in **1**. There is one word that you don't need.

course dear ~~great~~ here
just ready shame surprise

LISTENING

Activating background knowledge

1 a You are going to hear part of a travel programme about a relaxing holiday. Tick (✓) three topics you think you'll hear.

geography ____ survival ____
holiday activities ____ work ____
technology ____ weather ____

b 2.2 Listen and check.

2 a Write the three topics from **1** below. Add three words or expressions for each topic.

1 geography: beach ________ ________
2 ________: ________ ________ ________
3 ________: ________ ________ ________

b Listen again and check the words and expressions you hear.

STRATEGY Read the task before you listen. What do you know about this topic? Can you think of any useful topic words or expressions? Use your background knowledge to help you to predict key ideas and vocabulary in the recording.

Listening for specific information

3 Complete the summary with one word in each gap. Use the key ideas in the box to help you.

direction language place
temperature things month

CAYE CAULKER is an (1) island in the Caribbean, 50 kilometres (2) ________ of Mexico. The reviewer spent a holiday there last (3) ________. The island is unusual because there aren't any (4) ________ there. The reviewer also liked the fact that most of the locals speak (5) ________. The weather is sunny and (6) ________. On holiday, the reviewer swam in the sea, and relaxed on the (7) ________. She also enjoyed fishing, sailing, and watching the (8) ________.

STRATEGY Listen for key ideas to answer the questions. Remember: you do not need to understand every word that you hear!

WRITING Planning what to write

a I live in Tarifa, on the south coast of Spain. Last weekend, my husband and I went on a day trip to Africa! We took a boat to Tangiers, in Morocco.

b We spent the day sightseeing in Tangiers. It's a small city, but very busy. While we were exploring, my husband got lost! Luckily, we found each other again, after about half an hour!

c We spent ages in the medina (market), which was very bright and colourful. It was our favourite place. We loved the local street food – yoghurt with avocado is delicious!

d The streets were sometimes very busy and noisy. Also, some of the shops were quite expensive, so we didn't buy many souvenirs.

e Tangiers isn't a peaceful place, and you need a good map, but it's really exciting! I definitely recommend it for a day trip.

Pilar – New User ★★★★☆

1 **a** Read the review of a day trip. Did Pilar have a good time? Why/Why not?

b Read Pilar's notes. Circle the things that Pilar doesn't say in her review.

Tangiers – Morocco

great food *husband got lost!* *boring museum*
small and busy *lovely market* *expensive shops*
noisy *crowded beach* *went by boat* *very exciting*

2 **a** Read the review again. Match the topics in the box to paragraphs a–e of the review.

conclusion dislikes likes introduction what we did

Paragraph	Main topic	Notes
a		
b		
c		
d		
e		

b Complete the table for each paragraph with the notes from **1b**.

3 Plan a review of a day trip you went on last year, for example to a beach, a mountain, the countryside or a city. It can be a good or bad experience. Write notes about your trip and make a paragraph plan.

4 Write your review.

STRATEGY Always plan before you write. Follow these stages:
1 Write notes. 2 Choose your best ideas. 3 Decide which information to include in each paragraph.

3 ICONS

VOCABULARY
Landmarks

1 Complete the crossword with landmarks.

Across

3 A place that was a building. It is now destroyed so you can only see stones.

5 A very old religious building.

8 In Ancient Greece and Rome, people watched sports in this place.

9 A king or an emperor lives in this building.

Down

1 An area where people live. It is larger than a town.

2 A stone or metal figure of a person, often in a public place.

4 A figure of a person, an animal, or an object that a sculptor makes.

5 A tall building. At the top, you can see a long way.

6 You use this to walk over a river.

7 In the past, people built this around the outside of a city. There is a very famous one in China.

2 Circle the option that <u>doesn't</u> work.

1 They built a *statue* / *tower* / *wall* to defend the city.

2 There is a *palace* / *sculpture* / *statue* of our most famous composer in the main square.

3 In the past, an important place in the town was the *arena* / *ruins* / *temple*.

4 In my city the *tower* / *town* / *bridge* is a famous landmark.

5 The queen spent a lot of time in the *bridge* / *palace* / *temple*.

3 Choose the correct options to complete the conversation.

A Have you seen the (1)*designs / designers* for the new museum? It's going to be an amazing (2)*building / builder*.

B No, I haven't. What's it like? I know the (3)*architecture / architect* who planned it is very famous.

A There are a lot of huge windows, at the front. The chief (4)*engineer / engineering* says it will be difficult to build!

B I'm sure! But it will be a new landmark for the city. What will be inside the museum?

A There will be displays about famous artists and (5)*sculptors / sculptures*, I think.

4 a 3.1 **Listen to Masako and Jim. Number the places 1–5 in the order you hear them. There is one place that you don't hear.**

arena	____	statue	____
bridge	____	temple	____
palace	____	tower	____

b Complete the sentences. Listen again and check.

1 Many people think that Kyoto is the most beautiful city in Japan. It was the c____________ city in the past.

2 It's a very important religious m____________ in our country.

3 That building is Kyosho Gosho. It was a palace and it was built for the E____________ of Japan.

4 It's named in m____________ of a professor at the university.

5 People come here to bury the d____________ .

Cultural icons

5 Choose the correct option.

1 That woman's face looks *familiar / popular*. Do you think she was on TV?
2 If you star in a reality TV programme, you'll be *famous / iconic*!
3 Mick Jagger is the *familiar / legendary* singer of The Rolling Stones.
4 Did you know that a student designed the *iconic / popular* Nike 'tick' logo?
5 My granddad's a writer. He's not world-famous, but he is *legendary / well-known*.
6 Ms Nunan is the most *popular / well-known* teacher in the school. Everyone likes her.

6 Complete the sentences. Put the letters in the correct order.

1 Everybody knows Leo Messi. He's a __________ name. **DOOSHELHU**
2 Reality TV can make an ordinary person into a __________ . **CERYBTILE**
3 John Lennon was an __________ for the peace movement. **CONI**
4 Lady Gaga is so famous now that she is an international __________ . **UPETARRSS**
5 Nelson Mandela is already a __________ . **DELENG**

VOCABULARY EXTENSION
Celebrities

7 **a** Read the definitions and complete sentences 1–7 with the **bold** words.

A-list *(n)* a group of the most famous celebrities
autograph *(n)* a famous person's signature
bodyguard *(n)* a person who protects a famous person
limousine *(n)* a long, expensive car with many seats in it
paparazzi *(npl)* people who take pictures of celebrities for newspapers
VIP *(n)* a Very Important Person – a celebrity, a politician, etc.
wealthy *(adj)* very rich

1 The band arrived at the concert in a __________ .
2 Everywhere celebrities go, the __________ try to take photos of them.
3 You can only come into this part of the hotel if you are a __________ .
4 There's always a __________ with a gun near the president.
5 After I was on that TV show, everyone wanted my __________ .
6 World-famous movie stars are on the __________ – reality TV stars are on the D-list!
7 Many celebrities are extremely __________ – they have millions of dollars!

b 3.2 Listen and check.

BRING IT TOGETHER

8 Complete the words.

Gustave Eiffel

What connects the Statue of Liberty with France's (1) i _ _ _ _ c Eiffel Tower? They're both the work of French (2) e _ g _ _ _ e _ Gustave Eiffel. Eiffel didn't design Liberty, but he did plan the metal structure of the (3) s _ _ t _ e. Although he is now (4) f _ m _ _ s, Eiffel started at the bottom. When he left college, he had a small job working on (5) br _ d _ _ s for railways. Later, he started his own company and worked as an (6) a _ _ h _ te _ _ , making the plans for railway stations. His (7) b _ _ l _ _ _ gs were a great success. As his company became (8) p _ p _ _ _ r, he was asked to work on the Statue of Liberty. Finally, seven years later, he was called to Paris. The French capital city was holding the 1889 World's Fair and they wanted something special to attract visitors. Eiffel's idea was his legendary (9) t _ w _ _ . It immediately made Eiffel a (10) h _ _ s _ h _ _ _ name across the world, and it's still standing today, 130 years later – although the original plan was to destroy it after just twenty years!

GRAMMAR

Relative clauses

1 Circle the options that <u>don't</u> work.

Vienna's Hundertwasserhaus is one of the city's most famous landmarks – many of the tourists [(1)] *who / that / which* visit the Austrian capital make a special journey to see it. Here, Friedensreich Hundertwasser and Joseph Krawiner designed an amazing building [(2)] *that / who / which* provides homes for 200 people. Hundertwasser was an artist [(3)] *that / which / who* became famous in the 1950s for his crazy paintings. He also wanted to create buildings [(4)] *that / what / which* were both useful and beautiful, like Hundertwasserhaus. Hundertwasser was someone [(5)] *that / what / who* believed that nature is very important. For this reason, there are no straight lines in the building, because there are no straight lines in nature. It also has many balconies, with plants and trees growing. Hundertwasser called these plants 'tree tenants' – a tenant is a person [(6)] *what / which / who* rents an apartment. He believed the trees paid rent by providing clean air. These ideas were very unusual in 1986, when the building opened. Unfortunately, there was one problem: the building is too popular! The tenants [(7)] *that / which / who* live there have tourists looking at their flats all day. Every time they look out of their windows, they see people [(8)] *that / what / who* are taking photos of their homes!

2 Match 1–6 to a–f.

1 This is the statue ____
2 I'd like to speak to the man ____
3 Dave has a book ____
4 There were several visitors ____
5 An architect is someone ____
6 Here are the photos ____

a which contains a lot of information about the city.
b that designs buildings.
c that they took of the Burj Khalifa in Dubai.
d that I told you about.
e who were unhappy about the ticket prices.
f who was here yesterday.

Articles: *a/an, the,* no article

3 Complete the sentences with *a/an, the* or *0* (no article).

1 The notice says that ____________ children under 16 can't watch the film.
2 Can you help me? There's ____________ problem with my computer.
3 Where's ____________ shop which you showed me last weekend?
4 There's ____________ interesting building at the end of this street.
5 There's ____________ strange sign on the door and I don't know what it means.
6 It's the most famous landmark in ____________ city.
7 In this country, most people live in ____________ apartments.
8 Many tourists want to see ____________ main temple. It's 1,500 years old.
9 Do people have ____________ gardens in their homes in your country?
10 I'm trying to find ____________ taxi but I can't see any.

4 Add *a/an* or *the* where necessary.

1 A Nobody knows how to get to beach.

B We need to put up sign that shows them where it is.

2 A Is there internet café in this town?

B Yeah, it's at end of Hillman Road.

3 A I'm reading interesting book at the moment.

B Oh, is that book that Matt gave you?

4 A I really enjoyed our holiday. All campsites were great, weren't they?

B And tent was really comfortable too. I'm pleased we bought that one.

5 A That's strange building! What do you think it is?

B I don't know, but it looks like art gallery, or something like that.

5 Correct one mistake in each sentence.

1 The life is full of surprises.

2 There's an university in my home town.

3 Yvain doesn't eat the meat. He's a vegetarian.

4 Do you remember first time we went to Brussels?

5 Aztecs built some incredible buildings in Mexico.

6 We have the lunch in the school canteen at 12 every day.

7 There's new student in our class. Her name's Monique.

8 Sara loves the languages. She speaks English, Hindi and Arabic!

9 Did you know that there's a art gallery in the city centre?

10 Doctor told me that I need to relax.

BRING IT TOGETHER

6 Complete the text with one word in each gap. There are two gaps where no word is needed.

Men are from Mars

There are very few symbols (1) ________ people use all over (2) ________ world, but two of the most common ones are the symbols for male and female. So where do these two unusual images come from? Surprisingly, they are not (3) ________ invention from the twentieth century. The scientist (4) ________ first used these symbols to mean male and female was Carl Linnaeus: in 1751, when he was studying (5) ________ plant biology, Linnaeus used them to show if (6) ________ plant was male or female. Linnaeus copied these symbols from the Romans: they used the male symbol for the planet Mars and the female symbol for Venus. At (7) ________ time when Linnaeus lived, most scientists spoke (8) ________ Latin and so they knew these symbols well. They were a logical choice. The symbols were just one of Linnaeus's big ideas: he was a man (9) ________ completely changed the world of science. He also thought of the scientific names (10) ________ are now used for many species, including *homo sapiens*. So we can even thank Linnaeus for naming us!

FUNCTIONAL LANGUAGE Expressing preference

1 **a** Choose the correct option.

1 Which is *better* / *favourite*?
2 Which *one's* / *thing's* your favourite?
3 Which do you *prefer* / *rather*?
4 Wouldn't it be better to *get* / *getting* that one?

b 3.3 Complete the replies to the questions in **1**. Listen and check.

1 I much p__________ an interesting photo.
2 I__________ m__________ r__________ have something that's funny and makes me laugh.
3 I l__________ modern, trendy designs b__________ of all.
4 I l__________ classic, traditional images b__________ t__________ modern ones.

2 Listen again. Match speakers 1–4 to postcards a–d.

a ____

b ____

c ____

d ____

LISTENING Listening for gist

1 **a** 3.4 Listen to a podcast about fame. Tick (✓) the best description.

1 Two celebrities discussing the ways they became famous. ____
2 An interview with a celebrity giving advice on how to become famous. ____
3 An interview with an actress about how to write a famous book. ____
4 Two people discussing the mistakes people make when they're trying to become famous. ____

b Write <u>two</u> more things you remember from the podcast.

1 ______________________________
2 ______________________________

STRATEGY Listen for general understanding first. After you listen, try to summarise the most important ideas that you've heard. This will help you to understand better the next time you listen.

Listening for opinions

2 Listen again. Does Maruschka agree (✓) or disagree (✗) with these tips?

TOP TIPS

1 Be beautiful. *X*
2 Don't worry about what other people think. ____
3 Go on reality TV shows. ____
4 Have a celebrity boyfriend/girlfriend. ____
5 Work every day. ____
6 Post online videos. ____
7 Watch or read the news. ____

STRATEGY We often use expressions like *I think/agree* or *in my opinion* to give our opinions. Listen carefully for negative forms (with *don't*, *isn't*, etc.) which express disagreement.

READING Predicting content

1 a **Look at the photo and read the title of the profile. Decide if sentences 1–4 will be true (T) or false (F).**

1 Michael travels to different countries. T / F
2 Michael doesn't usually buy presents on holiday. T / F
3 Michael has an unusual hobby. T / F
4 Michael paints famous landmarks. T / F

b **Read the profile quickly and check.**

STRATEGY Looking at any photos and reading the title of a text can help you to predict the main ideas.

Michael Hughes (1952 –), photographer

Michael Hughes is a British photographer who emigrated to Germany in 1983. In 1999, Michael found a way to combine his favourite hobbies – photography and travelling – in a very original and exciting way. While he was visiting the Lorelei cliffs near the River Rhine, Michael bought a cheap picture postcard for his daughter. He held the card exactly in front of the view, and took a photo. His friends and family thought the photo was very funny, and they liked it more than the postcard. After that moment, Michael decided to photograph souvenirs in famous tourist destinations around the world.

Michael visited more than 50 countries, taking his camera as well as his passport on every trip. He photographed a cup in front of the Statue of Liberty, a pen stand at the Pyramids, and his daughter eating a tower-shaped sweet at the Tower of Pisa. Sometimes Michael visited these countries for work, or for a family holiday. But sometimes he visited them just to take a photograph!

His hobby quickly became a passion. Michael uploaded his favourite photos onto *Flickr*, and they soon became an internet hit. By 2006, his website had more than 5 million views. In 2008, Michael's pictures appeared in National Geographic magazine – he was famous! Michael now has more than 150 photos in his collection, his own book and online shop, and many thousands of fans. He also has *lots* of terrible souvenirs!

Using key words

2 a **Underline key words in questions 1–6.**

1 In which country was Michael born?
2 What are his main interests?
3 Who did Michael buy a present for in 1999?
4 What did Michael always take with him when he was travelling?
5 Where did Michael take a photo of a kind of food?
6 How many times did people look at Michael's photos online?

b **Read the profile again carefully and answer the questions in 2a. Underline the words in the profile which helped you.**

1 *in the UK* ______ 4 ______
2 ______ 5 ______
3 ______ 6 ______

STRATEGY When you need to answer questions about a text, first underline the key words in the questions. These are usually nouns, main verbs or important adjectives. Then look for words in the text which have a similar meaning. Remember, the text may not use exactly the same words.

PROGRESS TEST 1

GRAMMAR & VOCABULARY (25 points)

1 Choose the correct options to complete the email. *(10 points)*

Hi Lara,

I hope all's well! Janos and I are having an amazing holiday in New Delhi. Yesterday, we (1) *went / were going* to the Akshardham Temple. The temple (2) *opened / was opening* in 2005, so it isn't very old. But today it (3) *'s / 's being* the biggest Hindu temple in the world! While we (4) *visited / were visiting* the temple, we (5) *bought / were buying* some great souvenirs and cards. I (6) *sent / was sending* you a postcard this afternoon, when we (7) *waited / were waiting* for the bus back to the hotel. I hope you get it before we return! At the moment, I (8) *write / 'm writing* to you from our hotel room. Janos isn't with me – he (9) *exercises / 's exercising* in the gym. I (10) *think / 'm thinking* he's crazy – it's really hot here! Love to you and your family. Write soon!

Ilona

2 Complete the sentences with the words from the box. There are two gaps where no word is needed. *(4 points)*

a a the the which which who

1 New Delhi is __________ very big city. It's one of the ten biggest cities in __________ world. More than 18 million __________ people live there!
2 New Delhi is the place __________ Ilona and Janos visited on holiday. They really liked __________ Akshardham Temple.
3 Diwali, or 'the festival of lights', is an important Hindu festival __________ many __________ tourists go to see in New Delhi every year.
4 Roshan Seth is __________ successful actor from New Delhi __________ acts in both Indian and American films.

3 Circle the different word. *(6 points)*

1 Peru Kenya Mandarin Belgium
2 mountain inland island coast
3 statue architect designer sculptor
4 monkey zoo lion sheep
5 icon familiar popular legendary
6 speak talk listen tell

4 Complete the words. Then choose the answer which is right for you. *(5 points)*

1 Do you _ _ _ _ the newspaper every day? Yes / No
2 Do you _ _ _ _ friends round at the weekend? Yes / No
3 Do you _ _ _ _ the internet every day? Yes / No
4 Do you often eat _ _ _ at restaurants? Yes / No
5 Do you _ _ _ _ a lot of emails? Yes / No

READING (25 points)

1 Read the article quickly. What kind of text is it? *(2 points)*

a a factual description ____
b a personal opinion ____
c a travel review ____

Japanese Brazil

Brazil is home to the largest Japanese population in the world outside Japan. There are about 1.5 million people from Japanese families in Brazil today – that's around 0.8% of Brazil's total population. There are also around 300,000 Japanese Brazilians living in Japan.

The first 165 Japanese families travelled to Brazil in 1908 to work on the coffee farms. When the First World War began in 1914, many more families followed, and between 1917 and 1940 around 164,000 Japanese people moved to Brazil. Life for many was very difficult. Farm workers often worked long hours, for little money. What's more, very few of the first Japanese workers spoke Portuguese, and life in Brazil seemed very 'foreign'.

Today, Japanese Brazilians have a strong Brazilian identity. Most speak Portuguese as their first language, although many still speak Japanese with older relatives. Modern Japanese Brazilians work in all kinds of industries and have an important role in the life of Brazil. Famous Japanese Brazilians include the architect, Ruy Ohtake, who designed many landmark buildings in São Paulo, and the singer, Lovefoxxx, who is internationally famous.

Culturally, Brazil is now more 'Japanese' too. Many Brazilians enjoy eating Japanese food and celebrating Japanese festivals, like the *Tanabata Matsuri*, or 'star festival', in July. Some people also say that the Liberdade district of São Paulo looks like Tokyo!

2 Read the article again and complete the fact file. *(9 points)*

- Number of Japanese Brazilians – in Brazil: (1) __________, in Japan: (2) __________
- Date the first Japanese families arrived: (3) __________
- Number of Japanese people who moved between 1917 and 1940: (4) __________
- Main language – of first Japanese Brazilians: (5) __________, of modern Japanese Brazilians: (6) __________
- Two famous Japanese Brazilians: (7) __________, (8) __________
- Japanese district in São Paulo: (9) __________

3 Correct the wrong sentences. Tick (✓) two correct sentences. *(14 points)*

1 Nearly 2% of the people who live in Brazil are Japanese.
2 Some Japanese Brazilians moved back to Japan.
3 The first Japanese workers earned a lot of money.
4 Modern Japanese Brazilians never speak Japanese.
5 Ruy Ohtake is a famous Japanese Brazilian singer.
6 Japanese food is popular in Brazil.
7 People celebrate the 'star festival' in autumn.

LISTENING *(25 points)*

1 **a** T1 Listen to a radio programme about London. Tick (✓) the languages you hear. *(5 points)*

Arabic	☐	Mandarin	☐	English	☐
French	☐	Spanish	☐	Japanese	☐
Hindi	☐	Dutch	☐	Cantonese	☐

b Match the speakers to the languages they mention. *(6 points)*

Speaker 1 ______
Speaker 2 ______
Speaker 3 ______

2 Listen again and answer with the numbers from the box. There are two numbers that you don't need. *(14 points)*

87,000 13 million 23 350
1 million 1 41 8,700 2

1 the number of languages in London: ______
2 the number of Londoners who don't speak English at home: ______
3 the percentage of school students in London who don't speak English at home: ______
4 the number of official languages in Morocco: ______
5 the percentage of British people who speak some French: ______
6 the number of international students at London universities: ______
7 the number of international tourists who visit London every year: ______

WRITING *(25 points)*

1 Read the online review and complete the paragraph plan with the headings. There is one heading that you don't need. *(6 points)*

Reasons to visit
Landmarks
Places to stay
~~Geography and languages~~
The countryside

Paragraph 1	*Geography and languages*
Paragraph 2	
Paragraph 3	
Paragraph 4	

My review: Suriname

1 Suriname is a small country in South America. The capital city, Paramaribo, is on the north coast. The official language here is Dutch, but many other languages are also popular, like English and Hindi. It isn't a very big country, but I think it's beautiful.

2 There are lots of beautiful buildings in Paramaribo. If you have time, visit the huge, wooden cathedral, then the mosque and the synagogue. You should also explore the streets around the Presidential Palace, because the architecture there is really interesting. The city is a very friendly place, so it's great for tourists.

3 My favourite part of Suriname is the south, which has mountains and tropical rainforests. I visited the area last year with my family, and we had a wonderful time. We saw monkeys, snakes and birds while we were exploring the forests!

4 In my opinion, Suriname is perfect for people who enjoy having adventures and exploring exciting new destinations. It's unique – there's nowhere in the world like it!

2 Circle one example of *and*, *but*, *because*, *so*, and *then* in the review. Complete the sentences with the linkers. *(4 points)*

0 It's a beautiful, wild *and* exciting place.
1 It's very hot there, ______ bring sun cream!
2 First visit the church, ______ go to the temple.
3 The region is small, ______ it's never boring.
4 Don't miss the beach, ______ it's great for surfing.

3 Write a review of your country or region for tourists. Use the paragraph plan in **1** to help you. *(15 points)*

4 AGES AND CHANGES

VOCABULARY

Life stages

1 Complete the words.

1 Cristina's 19, so technically, she's still a t __ __ n __ __ __ r.
2 My grandma's a p __ n __ __ __ n __ r. She doesn't work now.
3 They say you're m __ d __ __ __ -a __ __ d in your 40s. Well, I'm 45 and I still feel young.
4 In my country, there's a card for y __ u __ __ a __ __ __ ts. It gives you cheap tickets on trains.
5 A c __ __ l __ can eat for free in the restaurant if they come with two adults.
6 My sister's just had a b __ __ __! Little Jacob was born last week.
7 I think you're an a __ __ __ t when you're 18.

2 Complete the text with the words from the box. There is one word that you don't need.

born died grew job
left married retired went

Arthur Ashe

Arthur Ashe was one of the greatest tennis players of the 1960s and 1970s. He was (1) __________ in Virginia, USA, in 1943. He grew up there and in St Louis, where he went to high school. In 1963, he (2) __________ home and started university. He (3) __________ to university in California, and after graduating he got his first (4) __________, in the US army. Three years later, in 1969, Ashe started to play tennis professionally. He was very successful. Ashe got (5) __________ to his wife in 1977, and they later adopted a daughter. Everything in his life looked good, until one day in 1979 when he had a heart attack. He (6) __________ from tennis the next year. But there was tragedy to come. When he had his heart problems, the hospital gave him blood containing HIV, and Ashe (7) __________ from AIDS in 1993 at the age of only 49.

3 Choose the correct option.

1 It's difficult for young people to *become* / *go* independent because house prices are very high.
2 My uncle and aunt *went* / *got* divorced. It was sad to see the end of their marriage.
3 Most children *learn* / *study* to walk and talk when they're about a year old.
4 My grandparents *got* / *had* three children: my dad and my two aunts.
5 What age do people *complete* / *finish* school in your country?
6 Traditionally, you *come* / *get* of age when you're 21.
7 I can *choose* / *vote* for the president for the first time this year.
8 How old were you when you *studied* / *went* to school for the first time?
9 Everyone in my school is learning to *drive* / *ride* a car.
10 Nick *became* / *fell* in love with a girl from his English course.

Activities

4 What is it? Complete the names of the activities.

1 It's a hobby where you make your own clothes with wool. k__________
2 It's a game where you try to move a little white ball into 18 different holes. g__________
3 It's an activity where you stand and move around on a piece of wood with four wheels. s__________
4 It's a sport where you fight another person. You wear white clothes with coloured belts. k__________
5 It's the most important instrument in a rock band. e__________ g__________
6 It's a sport where you try to catch, e.g. salmon in a river. f__________
7 It's an activity from Asia. You move your body into unusual positions. y__________

5 Circle the option that <u>doesn't</u> work.

1 Hiro plays *golf* / *karate* / *the violin* really well.
2 How often do you go *fishing* / *skateboarding* / *tennis*?
3 All the kids at my school do *golf* / *karate* / *crafts*.
4 You're not allowed to go *football* / *surfing* / *swimming* here.
5 Lots of people play *computer games* / *crafts* / *the electric guitar* in their free time.
6 Where do you usually play *football* / *the piano* / *yoga*?

Home life

6 Match 1–7 to a–g.

1 There are lots of jobs to do around the home. ____
2 We need to do the shopping. ____
3 We have to pay the bills. ____
4 It's time to do the housework. ____
5 I make the breakfast on Sundays. ____
6 We need someone to look after the children tonight. ____
7 I'm going to do some gardening this weekend. ____

a The electricity, the water, the gas, the internet – everything!
b Mum likes tea and toast in bed!
c I want to plant some vegetables.
d Can you ask your brother to come?
e We need to paint the living room and the hall.
f Let's go to the supermarket.
g I'll clean the kitchen and you do the bathroom.

VOCABULARY EXTENSION

Other home life words

7 Look at the pictures. Complete the sentences.

feed the cat

chill out

take out the rubbish

tidy up

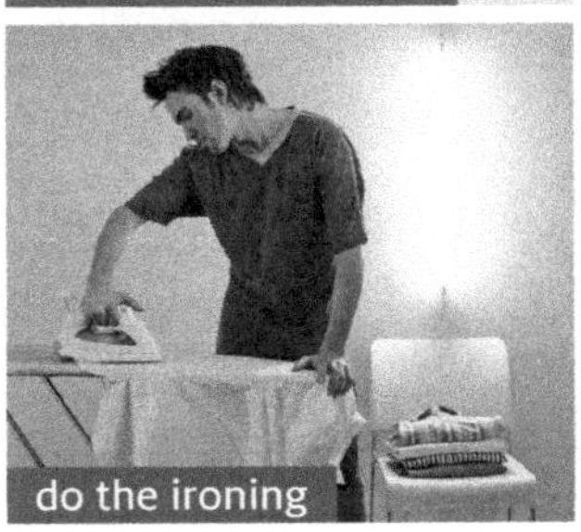
do the ironing

get the post

1 Danny, can you ______________________, please? It smells terrible!
2 There are 20 shirts here! I'll need hours to ______________________.
3 I'm going downstairs to ______________________. I'm waiting for an important letter.
4 Will you ______________________? There's a can of food in the kitchen.
5 Hans didn't have time to clean his office but he did ______________________ his desk before going on holiday.
6 I don't want to do anything today. I just want to ______________________ at home.

BRING IT TOGETHER

8 **a** 4.1 Listen to conversations 1–6. Decide if the speakers are happy (☺) or unhappy (☹).

1 ☺ ____ ☹ ____
2 ☺ ____ ☹ ____
3 ☺ ____ ☹ ____
4 ☺ ____ ☹ ____
5 ☺ ____ ☹ ____
6 ☺ ____ ☹ ____

b Correct one mistake in each conversation. Listen again and check.

1 A Harry! Can you help me do the housework, please?
B Sorry, Mum. I'm going out. I play karate on Saturday afternoons, remember?

2 C Everything's going well, thank you, Sue. My granddaughter got marry at the weekend.
D Did she? Who's the lucky man?

3 E I played fishing with my dad yesterday, and we caught an enormous fish. A salmon.
F Wow! Really? Are you going to cook it?

4 G Is something wrong, Kim?
H Yeah, my daughter left the home at the weekend to go to university.

5 I Are you enjoying the knitting class, Louise?
J No! It's too difficult for me. I'm not very good at playing crafts.

6 K Otto! I've got some news! My sister is going to have a baby!
L Great news! Congratulations, Bill. I didn't know they wanted to get children.

GRAMMAR

Present perfect

1 Write the past participles of the verbs.

1 do *done*
2 like *liked*
3 want ______
4 go ______
5 try ______
6 eat ______
7 have ______
8 play ______
9 teach ______
10 move ______
11 see ______
12 lose ______

2 Complete the conversation with the present perfect form of the verbs in brackets.

A (1) ______ you ever ______ (*teach*) someone a new skill?

B Yes, I have. I taught my friend to cook. She (2) ______ never ______ (*be*) good at cooking – she (3) ______ always ______ (*make*) convenience food!

A Really? Do you enjoy cooking then?

B Yes, I (4) ______ always ______ (*love*) cooking... and eating!

A Mm, I agree! What's the best thing you (5) ______ ever ______ (*eat*)?

B Wow, that's difficult. When Johan and I went to Thailand, we had delicious food. I (6) ______ always ______ (*not/like*) spicy food, but I loved the Thai curries we ate. I think that's the best food I (7) ______ ever ______ (*have*).

A Sounds fantastic! I (8) ______ (*not/go*) to Thailand, but I'd love to visit one day!

3 Complete the conversation with *always*, *ever* or *never*.

A Have you (1) ______ been fishing?

B Yes, I have. I've been with my uncle. He's (2) ______ loved fishing. What about you?

A No, I've (3) ______ tried fishing. I've (4) ______ wanted to – it doesn't interest me. I've (5) ______ played team sports instead.

Present perfect & past simple

4 Complete the conversations with one verb in the present perfect and one verb in the past simple.

1 A ______ (*you/ever/go*) to the USA?
B No, but we ______ (*go*) to Canada last year.

2 C ______ (*you/watch*) the new Almodóvar film on TV last night?
D No, but I ______ (*see*) it before. It's really good!

3 E Tim ______ (*live*) in his flat for over a year now.
F I know. I ______ (*help*) him move there last May.

4 G When ______ (*Silvio/start*) playing golf?
H When he was a child. He ______ (*always/love*) it.

5 I ______ (*the kids/drink*) all the orange juice? There isn't any in the fridge!
J Don't worry, I ______ (*buy*) some more yesterday. It's in the cupboard.

Present perfect with *for* & *since*

5 Choose the correct option.

1 Andrea has been a vegetarian for *seven years* / *2004*.
2 Nobody has sent me an email since *Monday* / *five days*.
3 Cameron's played the electric guitar in this band since *eight months* / *January*.
4 We haven't done any gardening for *a long time* / *last winter*.
5 Nobody in the class has had a birthday since *half a year* / *17 October*.
6 I haven't seen Theo for *last Tuesday* / *two weeks*.

Comparatives & superlatives

6 a Complete the sentences with the comparative form of the adjective in brackets.

1 The weather is ______ in Scotland than in my country. (*wet*)
2 I buy my newspaper here because the staff are ______ than in the other shop. (*friendly*)
3 Walking to work is ______ than taking the bus. (*quick*)
4 Which is ______ , the bus station or the train station? (*near*)
5 The exam today is ______ than the one tomorrow. (*important*)
6 My life is a lot ______ now that I have kids! (*busy*)
7 This new mobile phone is ______ than my old one. (*good*)
8 Playing the guitar is ______ than playing the piano. (*difficult*)
9 Oh dear! Your marks in Chemistry are ______ than your marks in Maths! (*bad*)
10 My brother Sven is ______ than me. (*young*)

b Put the adjectives in brackets from **6a** into these groups:

1 regular comparatives (one syllable adjectives):
______ ______ ______

2 regular comparatives (two syllables ending in *-y*):
______ ______

3 regular comparatives (two or more syllables):
______ ______

4 comparatives that double the last letter:
______

5 irregular comparatives: ______ ______

7 Complete the text with the superlative form of the adjectives from the box.

bad big easy lucky
noisy old small young

Today's question:
Is it bad to come from a large family?

Marcus (Switzerland)

I am 21 and the (1) ______ of six children (I'm the first). We had the (2) ______ family in my school – most people only had one brother or sister! I had the (3) ______ bedroom of all my friends – nice, but tiny! But I was the (4) ______ kid in my family because my brothers and sisters shared their rooms. I guess that's the (5) ______ thing about having a big family – you have to share everything! What does everyone think?

posted 11.24 AM

Posts (1)

Rita (Brazil !)

Hi Marcus! Your question is the (6) ______ one I've read today – I can answer in one word. No! Big families are great! I'm one of seven girls and I'm the (7) ______ – sometimes it's like having six mothers! But I love having a big family because there are always people in the house. Our house is the (8) ______ one in our street!

posted 2.59 PM

Bring it together

8 Choose the correct option to complete the blog post.

Belinda's Blog

Search:

Today has been the (1) *stranger / strangest* day so far in my trip to Poland. (2) *I've only been / I was only* here for a week, and I didn't know today is Dyngus Day... So, what happened? Since I arrived last Tuesday, I (3) *haven't had / didn't have* much time to explore, and today I got up (4) *earlier / earliest* than usual because I wanted to go sightseeing in Gdansk. But, when I left my apartment, this guy threw water over me, and then ran away! Teresa, my flatmate, came to help me. She was even (5) *more surprised / the most surprised* than me because the water was for her! This guy (6) *has wanted / wanted* to be Teresa's boyfriend for a long time, but she always says 'no'. So, he was waiting for Dyngus Day. People here have celebrated it (7) *for / since* 1,000 years. In the past, boys threw water over girls if they wanted to marry them. People still do it for fun, and I left my house at the (8) *worst / worse* possible moment – when this guy was waiting for Teresa!
But the (9) *funnier / funniest* thing happened this afternoon, when he came to say 'sorry'. Teresa waited on the balcony and then she (10) *threw / was throwing* water over him instead!

FUNCTIONAL LANGUAGE Catching up

1 4.2 Listen to the conversation. Where are Karina and Chavez?

2 a Correct mistakes 1–7 in the conversation.

A (1) Welcome again, Karina! *Welcome back, Karina!*
(2) I've miss you. ______

B Hi, Chavez! (3) It's great to look you again! ______
(4) So tell me, how's it go? ______

A Not bad, thanks! (5) What are things with you? ______

B Great, thanks! (6) I've got lots to say you. ______
(7) It's been a long time since we've last met! ______

A Let's go and have lunch. I want to hear everything!

b Listen again and check.

LISTENING Recognising context

1 a Complete the labels for photos a–e.

a ______ starting a new _ _ _

b ______ learning to _ _ _ _ _

c ______ leaving _ _ _ _

d ______ _ _ _ _ _ _ _ of age

e ______ _ _ _ _ _ _ _ in an election

b 4.3 Listen to five conversations. Match the conversations to photos a–e.

2 Listen again. Who says these things? Match them to conversations 1–5.

______ *Call me...*

______ *Congratulations!*

______ *Put your card in this box.*

______ *Slow down!*

______ *You're doing a great job.*

STRATEGY Try to work out why people are speaking. Who are the speakers? Where are they? What are they doing? Recognising the context can help you understand what the speakers are saying.

Checking answers

3 a Complete each sentence with one word.

1 Gabe wants to work as a ______ .
2 Christa goes past the ______ .
3 Christa parks behind the ______ car.
4 David works ______ than the last employee.
5 There are ______ names on Mrs Amusa's card.
6 Mrs Amusa will leave through the door on the ______ .
7 Mara's parents gave her a ______ .
8 Mara's cousin is ______ years older than her.

b Read and check that your completed sentences make sense. Listen again and check.

STRATEGY Always check your answers. Have you answered the task correctly? Do your answers look 'right'?

WRITING Punctuation

1 Read the two emails quickly.

Who...

1 has children? __________ 2 doesn't work? __________

Dear Stefan,

HAPPY CHRISTMAS!!!! I hope you have a great holiday! (1)its been a busy year for the Ceresole family Sylvain has finished school, and he's currently working for his dad at the garage. So now there are two mechanics in the family! (2)monique left university in july, and she got married to mathias in the autumn. The wedding was in Germany, because that's where Mathias is from. (3)luckily, everyone in his family also speaks good french We all like Mathias very much. (4)hes kind intelligent and very good-looking! We've also bought a new house. (5)It's close to lake geneva. (6)It's garden is enormous! (7)pierre and i have a lot of gardening to do next year. ☹ (8)how are you doing. Let's meet up soon!

Love,

Isabel

Post: Messages • Status • Photos • Videos •

Dear Dania,

GONG XI FA CAI!

Happy Chinese New Year to you and your family. I hope it brings you lots of happiness. Yuqi and I have enjoyed a wonderful year. We both retired in May, and since then we've been on a very long holiday. In three months, we've travelled to the UK, France, Italy and Greece, then across Asia to Australia. We're currently celebrating the New Year with my sister Zhang in Sydney. Have you ever been to Sydney? It's famous for its opera house. It's beautiful! Unfortunately, Zhang hasn't had a good year. She got divorced in the summer, and I think she's found it difficult. But we hope for good news soon.

Love to you and your family,

Wang

2 Read the rules. Then read Wang's email again and find one example of each rule.

We use:	
Capital letters (A, B, C)	• at the beginning of sentences. • for the personal pronoun *I*. • for the names of people, places, days, months, languages and nationalities.
. ! and ?	• at the end of sentences or questions.
Commas (,)	• for pauses and to separate words in a list. *He has short, black, curly hair.*
Apostrophes (')	• with informal contractions and to indicate possession. (*isn't, John's*) • Remember! *It's* (= *It is*) *my dog.* BUT *Its name is Millie.*

3 Rewrite sentences 1–8 in Isabel's email using the correct punctuation.

1 *It's been a busy year for the Ceresole family.*
2 __________
3 __________
4 __________
5 __________
6 __________
7 __________
8 __________

4 Write an email to a friend who you haven't seen for six months. Tell him/her what you have done since you last saw him/her.

STRATEGY Remember to use the correct punctuation, even in informal emails and letters.

5 LIVE AND LEARN

VOCABULARY
Education & learning

1 Complete the crossword with academic subjects.

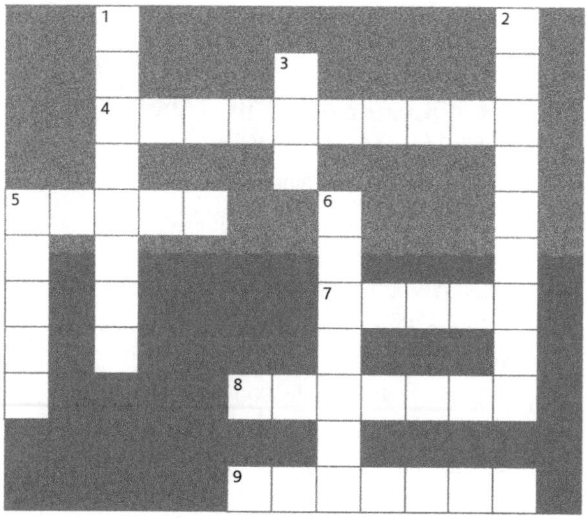

Across

4 This is the study of important books by great writers.
5 This is where you add (+), subtract (–), divide (÷) and multiply (×).
7 You play football, tennis, etc. in this lesson.
8 You learn about plants and animals in this class.
9 This is a type of science. Albert Einstein studied it.

Down

1 In this class, you learn about governments and leaders.
2 In this class, you do experiments with oxygen, iron, etc.
3 You draw and paint in this lesson.
5 This is where students learn to play the guitar, the piano or other instruments.
6 In this class, you read about important events in the past.

2 Complete the words.

1 I'm learning to be an electrician at a t _ _ h _ _ _ a _ college.
2 My three-year-old is starting p _ _-s _ _ _ _ l next week.
3 You need a lot of money to go to a u _ _ v _ _ _ i _ y like Harvard or Yale.
4 Children are about 12 years old when they start s _ _ _ n _ _ _ y school.
5 Your first school is usually a p _ _ _ _ ry school.
6 When you're 14 or 15, you start h _ _ _ school.
7 My kids are four and five so they're still at k _ _ d _ _ g _ _ _ _ _ _.

3 Complete the sentences. Put the letters in the correct order.

1 After my first degree, I decided to do a __________ in translation. **RESSAMT**
2 When you complete your education, you get a school __________ certificate. **GELVANI**
3 I got a professional __________ in web design. **LIDMOAP**
4 It's a good idea to get a __________ qualification in a subject like nursing. **CATLOONIVA**
5 I went to university for three years to get my __________. **EEGRED**

4 **a** 5.1 Listen to six conversations. Match the conversations to the academic subjects.

Business Studies	____	Languages	____
Geography	____	Drama	____
Information Technology	____	Philosophy	____

b Listen again. Complete the sentences.

1 I studied Plato on my __________ course at university.
2 But she's only six years old! She's at __________ school.
3 He's doing a __________ in Economics. It's a one-year course.
4 We're going to do a performance at the __________ school!
5 Is she going to study programming at __________ when she leaves school?
6 You're learning some interesting things now you're at __________ school.

-ed/-ing adjectives

5 Choose the correct option.

1 I don't understand the Physics homework. I'm *confused / confusing*!
2 We had a really *bored / boring* History lesson today.
3 I worked on my Geography project all last night. I'm really *tiring / tired* today!
4 We watched a *fascinated / fascinating* programme about Psychology yesterday.
5 Marco is the most *annoying / annoyed* student in the class. He talks all the time!
6 I try to teach my English students about literature but they're not *interesting / interested*.
7 Simone's really *excited / exciting* because she's starting her degree course next week.
8 I think Monday mornings are really *depressed / depressing*!

Adjectives + prepositions

6 Choose the correct option.

1 We're bored *about* / *with* doing the same thing every day.
2 They're really excited *about* / *at* the school trip to Paris.
3 I'm pretty good *at* / *in* Chemistry. It's my best school subject.
4 Are you interested *about* / *in* Psychology?
5 Maths is quite similar *to* / *with* Physics.
6 The lessons in secondary school are quite different *from* / *of* the ones in primary school.
7 He's very bad *at* / *with* sports. He can't run very fast.

VOCABULARY EXTENSION Education

7 Match the words in **bold** to definitions a–f.

1 I got really good **marks** in all my exams.
2 The **lecturer** on my Advanced Chemistry course is a world-famous professor.
3 Your final mark for this subject will come from your **coursework** and your end-of-year exams.
4 I didn't go to bed last night because I had to **revise**.
5 In American universities, there are two semesters, but in British ones there are three **terms**.
6 In my spare time, I go to an **evening class** to study Art.

a Numbers (e.g. 50%) or letters (e.g. A, B, C) that show the results of school work.
b A part of the school year. It's usually several weeks long.
c The homework, exercises and projects that you do while you are studying something.
d A teacher at a university.
e A course that you do after school or work.
f To read and study all your notes in preparation for an exam.

8 a Complete the sentences with the correct form of the words in **bold** from **7**.

1 What's the best way to __________ for exams?
2 If you're bored with your job, you should go to an __________ __________ to learn some new skills.
3 There are three __________ on my History course: Dr Smith, Mr Wei and Professor Bull.
4 Roger got great __________ in the exams – all A's!
5 You only have exams once a year, at the end of the summer __________ .
6 We do __________ all the time, and exams at the end of the year.

b 5.2 Listen and check.

BRING IT TOGETHER

9 Complete the text with the words from the box. There is one word that you don't need.

about annoyed at boring English fascinating from in Maths marks primary

TEACHER'S PET!

When parents take their kids to school, they don't expect to see a dog in the classroom. But some (1) __________ and secondary schools have found that dogs are good (2) __________ helping students to learn and improve their (3) __________ . Dogs are often used in (4) __________ classes to help students with their reading and writing. As one expert explains, 'Having a dog in the classroom is great for children who usually find reading (5) __________ or difficult. Reading to a dog is different (6) __________ reading to another student or a teacher – the dog doesn't get (7) __________ if a child reads slowly or makes mistakes! This helps the child relax and enjoy what they are reading.' Some teachers also use the dogs as a subject in their lessons. For example, students can practise (8) __________ by adding amounts of dog food.

Eric Brown, a teacher from the USA, started taking his dog Betty to classes last year. 'I'm really surprised. The children are always excited (9) __________ having Betty in the classroom but she doesn't distract them. They are actually much calmer and quieter when she's here! This has been a (10) __________ experience for me.'

GRAMMAR

Present continuous & *going to*

1 a Match a–b to i–ii.

1 a We're going to learn to speak Japanese ____
b We're studying the past tense in our Japanese class ____
i tonight.
ii when we retire.

2 a He's going to look for a new job ____
b He's starting his new job ____
i at 11 a.m. tomorrow.
ii soon.

3 a We're going to fly around the world ____
b We're flying to Greece ____
i when we have enough money.
ii tomorrow morning.

4 a I'm going to buy a new car ____
b I'm washing the car ____
i some day.
ii after lunch.

5 a They're going to move to Italy ____
b They're moving to Italy ____
i in July.
ii one day.

6 a She's not going to be a lecturer ____
b She's not meeting her lecturer ____
i until 12.
ii when she finishes the course.

b Which sentences in 1a are:

1 fixed plans? ________
2 general plans? ________

2 a 5.3 Alex has asked his friends to go out this evening. Listen to mobile messages 1–5.

Which person, 1–5,

a doesn't make a decision? ____
b has an evening class? ____
c has to look after his/her children? ____
d is revising for an exam? ____
e agrees to meet Alex? ____

b Complete the sentences. Listen again and check.

1 I ____________ my kids after kindergarten, then it's dinner time, bath time.
2 I want to come out. Where ________ we ____________ meet?
3 I don't know where I ____________ this evening. I'll call or text you or something.
4 Judy and I ____________ our Art class tonight from six to eight. But we're free after that.
5 I ____________ in the library this evening, all evening, so I can't meet this time.

Must(n't) & *(don't) have to* for obligation

3 Match 1–7 to a–g.

1 To be a chef in a restaurant, you must ____
2 To be a doctor you have ____
3 An Art teacher has ____
4 If you want to study IT, you must ____
5 In some countries, all shops have ____
6 When you go into a Japanese home, you must ____
7 All children must ____

a to know a lot about artists, paintings, etc.
b to close on Sunday.
c do a vocational qualification in cooking.
d be interested in computers.
e go to school until they are 16.
f take your shoes off.
g to study at university for about five years.

4 Choose the correct option.

1 Hotel guests *don't have to / mustn't* smoke in their rooms – it's not permitted.
2 Users *don't have to / mustn't* put a photo on their web page, but it is a good idea.
3 My sister *doesn't have to / mustn't* study a foreign language at her school – they're an option.
4 Passengers *don't have to / mustn't* take liquids on the plane. It's not allowed.
5 Your son *doesn't have to / mustn't* take more than six pills every day. That's the maximum.
6 I *don't have to / mustn't* wear a suit to work. I can wear jeans if I like.

5 Put the words in the correct order to make sentences.

1 finish have you to coursework your

____

2 school mustn't mobile in use phone you your

____

3 don't this have we pay for to evening class

____

4 must pencil bring to exam students a the

____

5 to don't to university go I have

____

6 Correct one mistake in each conversation.

1 A Can I see your identity card, please?
B Sorry?
A In this country, people must to show their identity card when they buy something by credit card.
B OK. Here's my passport.

2 C You don't have to tell Gianni about the party. It's a secret. OK?
D OK. I won't say anything.

3 E What time does Steven have to get to the airport?
F He musts be there two hours before the flight. So about 7 a.m.

4 G Oh, this is an interesting email...
H Hey! What are you doing? You don't must open an email if you don't know where it comes from.

5 I Turn off your mobile phone in this part of the hospital!
J Why do we has to do that?
I It can affect the machines.

6 K I'm sorry but we has to close the museum now.
L Oh, right. Where's the exit?
K It's over there, on the left.

BRING IT TOGETHER

7 Complete the text with the words and phrases from the box.

are don't have to going to (x2) has to I'm is must (x2) musn't

Game Ranger Course

This week, we (1)__________ doing the Game Ranger course at the Kruger National Park in South Africa. Like many people on the course, we aren't (2)__________ change our jobs and become rangers. Instead, we just want to learn about everyday life in the park. The course (3)__________ starting this afternoon!

On the course, students discover what the rangers actually do. It's essential that park rangers understand everything about the animals and their environment. A ranger often (4)__________ count the animals to know how many of each species are in the park. Also, they (5)__________ allow diseases to spread in the park, so the rangers (6)__________ know when the animals are sick. They are (7)__________ teach all of these things on the course.

The course entry requirements are simple. You (8)__________ be over 17 and have a driving licence. However, you (9)__________ have work experience as a ranger: the course is for complete beginners. That's all for now. (10)__________ going to write a full report when I get back in two weeks' time.

FUNCTIONAL LANGUAGE
Sounding polite

1 **a** Look at the photos. Which person do you think is the most polite?

b Match requests and replies 1–8 to the photos.

1 I want the salad. _____

2 Can I have the salad, please? _____

3 Give me that too. _____

4 OK. Whatever. _____

5 What would you like? _____

6 Of course. No problem. _____

7 Certainly. _____

8 Please could I have some water? _____

2 Rewrite more politely.

1 We want two tickets.
Could we have two tickets, please?

2 What do you want for dinner?
_____

3 Give us some money for the bus.
_____

4 The shop is closed.
_____

LISTENING Inferring relationships

1 5.4 Listen to three conversations. Tick (✓) the topic they have in common.

Studies and training _____
Work and careers _____
Favourite subjects and interests _____

2 **a** How do the speakers know each other? Listen again and match conversations 1–3 to three of the relationships.

sister and brother _____
sports star and interviewer _____
cousins _____
manager and assistant _____
teacher and student _____
doctor and patient _____

b Write two or three key words for each conversation which helped you in **2a**.

Conversation 1
_____

Conversation 2
_____

Conversation 3
_____

STRATEGY Working out the relationships between speakers can help you understand better. Listen for register (is this an informal or formal conversation?) and key topic words. Remember, some key words can be misleading, so always listen carefully to the whole recording!

Listening for specific information

3 Listen again and choose the correct option to complete the sentences.

Conversation 1 The woman's best subjects were
a Maths and Languages.
b Languages and History.
c Sport and Languages.
d Maths and Sport.

Conversation 2 The man's weakest skill is
a reading. b speaking.
c writing. d listening.

Conversation 3 The woman thinks that the main secret to success is
a hard work. b luck.
c skill. d confidence.

READING Matching information

1 Read the article about three people, Logan, Gosia and Malik, who changed careers. Match jobs a–f to the people.

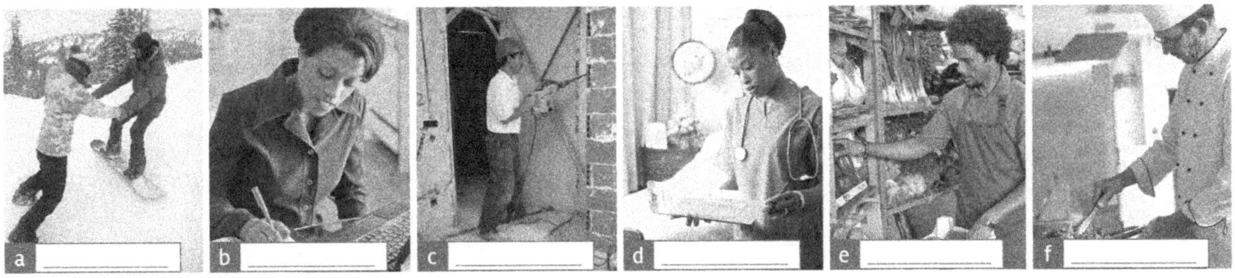
a ______ b ______ c ______ d ______ e ______ f ______

Bored with your job?

Then try something new! These people did…

1 › Logan

After a back injury, working on houses became impossible. I've always loved cooking for my family, so I decided to make my hobby a career. But my new job isn't easy. On building projects, I didn't have to work long hours. Now I often start work when it's still dark, and I have to work most evenings. A lot of the kitchen assistants are Mexican, so next month, I'm starting a Spanish course. But I don't know when I'm going to study!

2 › Gosia

In many ways, this is a dream job. I love winter sports and now I help others to enjoy my hobby. I have a late lie-in every day and the work is never boring. I meet interesting people from all round the world – luckily, I also speak French and German! But I miss the hospital. Helping sick people isn't as 'fun', but it feels more worthwhile. I'm going to return there in March. My brothers think I'm mad!

3 › Malik

I left school with just one qualification, in English Literature. After that, I worked in my parents' store. I was bad at selling groceries, but I loved chatting to customers. In my free time, I used their stories for my first book. Amazingly, a lot of people bought it, and it was a best-seller! My new job isn't perfect. On bad days, I stare at the computer for hours, with nothing interesting to say. But I've never wanted to work at the store again!

2 Read the article again. Answer the questions with Logan (L), Gosia (G) or Malik (M).

Who...

1 is going to do their old job again? ______
2 doesn't have to get up early? ______
3 has had a medical problem? ______
4 has worked with relatives? ______
5 is going to study a new language? ______
6 is sometimes bored in their new job? ______

STRATEGY When you have to match information to different texts, read all the texts carefully. Remember, the texts may say the same things in a different way, so don't just look for key words.

Guessing unknown words

3 **a** Find these words in the text. For each word, write adjective (A), noun (N) or verb (V).

1 dark (Logan) ____
2 worthwhile (Gosia) ____
3 best-seller (Malik) ____
4 stare (Malik) ____

b Choose the correct definitions for the words in **3a**. Read the whole sentence they appear in for clues.

1 *not light / very late*
2 *enjoyable, exciting / good, useful*
3 *very expensive book / very successful book*
4 *look for a long time / look very quickly*

STRATEGY When you find a word you don't know in a text, read the whole sentence carefully. Is the word an adjective, a noun or a verb? Then look at the context again and try to guess the meaning.

6 HELP!

VOCABULARY
Help

1 Match 1–11 to a–k.

1 The ambulance driver ______
2 The breakdown service took me home ______
3 Phone 112 in Europe ______
4 My mum's a charity worker – ______
5 An old man fell over in the road ______
6 The doctors at the hospital ______
7 The firefighter entered ______
8 A police officer came to speak to my dad ______
9 We need volunteers ______
10 If you are ill, ______
11 All the country's rescue workers are helping ______

a but luckily a passer-by phoned for help.
b because someone stole our car.
c the burning house to rescue the children.
d to help clean the city centre for free.
e there is a national health helpline that you can call.
f during the floods.
g drove very fast to the hospital.
h because there was a problem with my car.
i she helps homeless people.
j were very helpful after my brother's accident.
k to talk to the emergency services.

2 a Find six *-less* words in the word search.

H	O	M	E	L	E	S	S
X	C	Q	T	M	O	G	Q
F	A	W	U	K	E	H	O
Z	R	P	S	C	N	O	X
K	E	X	E	Z	D	P	F
W	L	G	L	H	L	E	G
P	E	K	E	X	E	L	G
S	S	E	S	D	S	E	K
S	S	T	S	M	S	S	C
J	D	W	J	H	G	S	J
H	E	L	P	L	E	S	S
O	T	Q	C	Z	B	B	M

b Complete the sentences with the words from **2a**.

1 The passer-by was ____________ – he couldn't do anything to stop the accident.
2 The police officer said that ____________ driving can be dangerous.
3 I've had ____________ problems with this car. I'm always calling the breakdown service!
4 This charity provides help for ____________ people.
5 I think this helpline is a good idea. But if nobody ever answers the phone, it's ____________ !
6 Doctors and police officers have to stay calm in an emergency – I'd be ____________ at that.

3 Complete the *-ful* words.

1 You need to be c____________ when you use a knife.
2 I sent Xue-li's present last week so I'm h____________ that it'll arrive in time for her birthday.
3 These emails never contain any u____________ information.
4 The police officer gave us directions. She was very h____________ .
5 I'm so g____________ to all the nurses in the hospital. They looked after me very well.

Senses

4 a Complete each pair of sentences with the correct form of one word from the box.

feel look smell sound taste

1 a I like your sunglasses. They ____________ very cool.
b Preeti ____________ stunning on her wedding day.
2 a Your voice ____________ strange. Have you got a sore throat?
b I didn't enjoy the concert last night. The band ____________ awful!
3 a Your trainers ____________ terrible. You really need to clean them.
b That curry ____________ great. I can't wait to try some!
4 a I love these new shoes. They ____________ really comfortable.
b It ____________ really hot in here. Can I open a window?
5 a I can't drink this coffee. It ____________ too strong.
b These lemon cakes ____________ delicious!

b 6.1 Listen and check.

Health problems

5 Complete the puzzle. What is the hidden word?

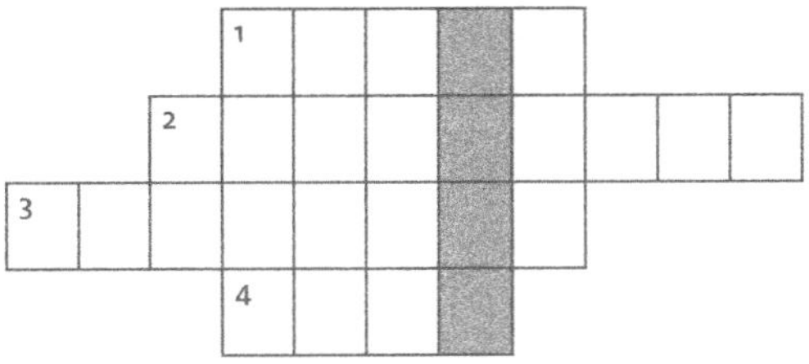

1 If you ___________ your leg, you can't walk for a few weeks.
2 An ear ___________ can be very painful.
3 If you have a ___________ , you should take a painkiller.
4 I have a really ___________ throat today.

6 Complete the sentences.

1 My back really hurts. I'm going to take a p___________ .
2 When you have an infection, it's a good idea to drink l___________ .
3 If your tooth is hurting, you might need to see a d___________ .
4 When I broke my arm, I had to have an X-___________ .
5 You need to s___________ a doctor about that red mark on your skin.
6 You have an infection. You need to s___________ in bed for the next couple of days.
7 You've recovered from the illness but you shouldn't go out. You need to r___________ .

Vocabulary extension

Other health problems

7 Match the words from the box to definitions 1–6.

backache cold depression flu stomachache toothache

1 This is a very common illness. It can cause a sore throat and sneezing. ___________
2 This can be very painful. Resting, taking a painkiller or doing yoga can help. ___________
3 Eating food that is not fresh can cause this problem. ___________
4 This is an emotional illness which can make you feel very sad and lonely. ___________
5 Many people get this illness in winter. They often have to stay in bed for a few days. ___________
6 This type of pain can be the result of eating too many sweet or sugary foods. ___________

Bring it together

8 Put the letters in the correct order to complete the text.

Heavy snow causes problems in the UK

The British police were furious yesterday when a woman phoned 999 – the phone number for the British emergency (1) ___________ (SSEECRIV). The woman (2) ___________ (DONDESU) angry because the snowman in her garden had disappeared. She wanted a police (3) ___________ (CERIFOF) to come to her house! The police were angry because, in the bad weather, (4) ___________ (LABAMUECN) drivers and other (5) ___________ (USECER) workers were very busy. As one driver told us, 'When it's snowy, many people fall and (6) ___________ (RAEBK) their legs or arms and they need to see a (7) ___________ (ROCTOD). It's a very busy time for us. Most people are really (8) ___________ (TELGAFRU) for the help we give, so stories like this are very frustrating. A phone call about a stolen snowman might sound funny. But you cannot call the (9) ___________ (PLEHENLI) if there are lots of other people on the phone. A (10) ___________ (RECASSLE) call can mean that other people don't get the help they need.'

GRAMMAR Modal verbs: *can/can't, should/shouldn't*

1 Complete the sentences with *can/can't* and the verbs from the box.

do help go teach tell ~~understand~~ use watch

1 I *can't understand* the sign because I don't speak Russian.
2 Svetlana __________ to her swimming class because she's got an ear infection.
3 I love working for this charity because I __________ people in my community.
4 I __________ my Maths homework. It's too difficult.
5 Milos __________ the film in the cinema because he isn't 18.
6 Excuse me, __________ you __________ me how to get to the station? I'm lost!
7 Nina __________ you how to ski because she's a ski instructor.
8 Guests __________ the computers in hotel reception to check their emails.

2 Choose the correct options to complete the blog post.

LETTER OF THE WEEK

I had to write because I have a problem – and I want people to understand it. I live on my own, and I am in a wheelchair, which means that I (1) *can / can't* walk around like everybody else. But that's not my problem. I (2) *can / can't* look after myself. I (3) *can / can't* cook, clean the house and do everyday things. But what I (4) *can / can't* accept is when people don't tell me the truth. For example, if I go out with my friends, I always phone the bar, restaurant or club first to find out if disabled people (5) *can / can't* move around it easily. People often say, 'Oh yes, disabled people (6) *can / can't* come here – we have special toilets, etc.' But when I arrive, I often (7) *can / can't* get in – because there are stairs in front of the door! Then my friends have to carry me inside. OK, they (8) *can / can't* do that... but I don't really want them to help me. Why don't people just tell me that there's a problem before I arrive?

Paul, Manchester

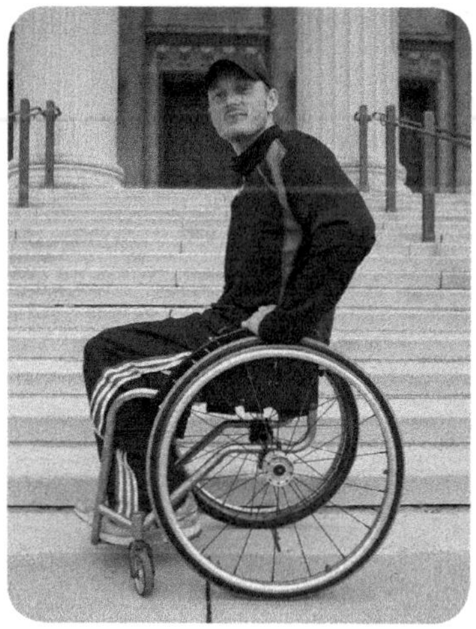

3 Choose the correct options to complete the interview.

INTERVIEWER This week we speak to American ambulance driver, Gene Colville. Gene, to be an ambulance driver, what kind of training (1)*should / shouldn't* you have?

GENE You don't need medical training because you get that on the job. But you (2)*should / shouldn't* be a careful driver.

INTERVIEWER Can you drive at any speed?

GENE No! In this state, an ambulance driver (3)*should / shouldn't* drive faster than the speed limit. That's about 55 miles per hour here. Also, we (4)*should / shouldn't* stop at red lights – in an emergency, we can drive through them, but we (5)*should / shouldn't* do that before all the other drivers know we are there.

INTERVIEWER Can you use your siren at all times?

GENE You (6)*should / shouldn't* use the siren all the time because it's bad for the person in the back of the ambulance. They feel frightened when they hear it. So you (7)*should / shouldn't* only use it when you really need it.

INTERVIEWER OK. And what kind of person (8)*should / shouldn't* you be?

GENE At an accident scene, ambulance drivers (9)*should / shouldn't* take action quickly. And people are often upset after an accident, so you (10)*should / shouldn't* be angry or nervous. Always be calm!

INTERVIEWER Gene, thank you.

Predictions: *will, may, might*

4 Correct one mistake in each sentence. Tick (✓) two correct sentences.

1 I think it will raining tomorrow.

______

2 We not might go out this weekend.

______

3 They won't phone you until Tuesday.

______

4 Jurgen wills go to university when he finishes school.

______

5 I may buy a newspaper at the station.

______

6 Mr Greene might to teach the new course next year.

______

5 Complete the text with *will/won't* or *may/might (not)*.

Do you want to help people in your local area? Have you thought about becoming a volunteer friend?

What do volunteers do?

Volunteer friends visit people in their area, giving them friendship and support. You (1) ______ visit a family, an elderly person, or someone with a disability. You (2) ______ just talk to them, or you (3) ______ help them with simple jobs like cooking or using a computer. These things (4) ______ seem important, but they (5) ______ make a big difference to your new friend!

Who can volunteer?

An ideal volunteer (6) ______ be good at listening and (7) ______ have about 2–3 free hours a week. He/She (8) ______ have experience, but this isn't important.

How do we help?

We understand that, at first, you (9) ______ feel confident about volunteering. But don't worry! We (10) ______ give you full training before you start. We (11) ______ ask you to do anything you're not sure about and we (12) ______ always help if you have any questions or problems.

For more information, or to find a 'friends' scheme near you, visit www.becomeafriend.com.

BRING IT TOGETHER

6 Choose the correct options to complete the web chat.

RAY Hi Selene! (1) *Can / Will* you chat now? I need help!

SELENE Sure! What's the problem?

RAY It's my son, Nick. He's unemployed and he's depressed. He applies for lots of jobs but gets no replies. He thinks he (2) *should / may* never get work.

SELENE Don't panic! It (3) *can / should* take a long time to find a job!

RAY So what's your advice?

SELENE Firstly, he (4) *may / should* tell everyone he knows that he's looking for a job.

RAY He (5) *shouldn't / won't* do that because he gets embarrassed.

SELENE Well, we all need help sometimes. And one of his friends (6) *might / will* know someone with a job offer – it's possible.

RAY OK.

SELENE And he (7) *may not / shouldn't* worry if people don't reply to his emails or calls. That's normal. People are busy and they (8) *can't / shouldn't* reply to every email – there just isn't time!

RAY Good advice.

SELENE Also, go to lots of conferences and trade fairs. He (9) *can't / might not* want to do that, but it is a really good way to meet people. People (10) *might / will* always react differently to you if they have met you face to face. Then you're a person, not just an email address.

RAY Thanks, Selene. That really helps.

FUNCTIONAL LANGUAGE Advice

1 Put the words in the correct order to complete the conversations.

Conversation 1

A I've only had four customers today!
(1) *What should I do?*
(I what do should ?)

B (2) ______
(advertise should you) Then more people will know about the restaurant.
(3) ______
(call why the local newspaper you don't ?)

Conversation 2

A I feel tired all the time.
(4) ______
(should I see think do a doctor you ?)

B (5) ______
(go to you need to earlier bed !)
Try that for a week and see how you feel.

Conversation 3

A I'm so stressed at the moment – I can't relax.
(6) ______
(should do what I ?)

B (7) ______
(yoga what about doing ?)
I'm sure that will help.

2 **a** 6.2 Listen and check your answers to **1**.

b Match conversations 1–3 to photos a–c.

a ______

b ______

c ______

3 Write one more piece of advice for the people in **1**.

Conversation 1
What about...

Conversation 2
______

Conversation 3
______

LISTENING

Listening for specific information

1 6.3 Tiago is organising a street party tonight, to raise money for charity. Listen. How many people phone him?

2 Listen again. Are the sentences true (T) or 'we don't know' (?)?

1 A journalist is going to write about it. ______
2 The street party will raise $1,000 for charity. ______
3 Guests don't have to wear formal clothes. ______
4 It finishes at eleven o'clock. ______
5 There's going to be music. ______
6 It starts at half past seven. ______
7 There's going to be food and drink. ______
8 It's near Green Road. ______

Inferring emotion

3 **a** Match emotions 1–6 to expressions a–f.

1 angry — c	a I'm quite busy at the moment.
2 excited	b I'm sorry, I don't understand.
3 sympathetic	c You shouldn't do that!
4 worried	d What should I do?
5 confused	e Wow. That's great news!
6 bored	f Oh no! That's awful.

b Listen again. For each call, choose the best emotion in **3a** to describe Tiago's response.

1 ______ 2 ______ 3 ______

STRATEGY To understand a speaker's emotions, listen carefully to what they say and how they say it (their intonation). Do they sound excited, angry, etc.? We often use exaggerated intonation to express strong emotion and flatter intonation to give factual information, or to express boredom.

WRITING Linkers: addition & sequence

1 Read the advert and Alba's email. How many questions does Alba ask?

News | Reply | Reply all | Forward | Delete

To: volunteering@music4life.charity.org

Hi,

I am interested in volunteering at the Music4Life Festival. I live near St Mary's, and I would like to help this important local hospital. **What's more**, I am **also** passionate about music, so I think I would really enjoy the festival **too**.

I would be grateful if you could send me more information. **Firstly**, could you tell me where the festival is going to be? **Secondly**, I'd like to know what kind of work volunteers can do. Unfortunately, I cannot sing or play music, but I am good at helping people. I can **also** cook, and I have experience of working in a shop **as well**. **Finally**, I would like to know if volunteers have to have any qualifications.

Thank you very much for your help.

Alba Villanova

Can you help?

Music4Life is a charity music festival, raising money for St Mary's hospital.

For more information, please contact us at:
volunteering@music4life.charity.org

2 **a** Look at the linkers in **bold** in Alba's email. Choose the correct option to complete the rules.

We use:	
Adding ideas	• **what's more** at the (1) *beginning* / *end* of a sentence. • **too** and **as well** at the (2) *beginning* / *end* of a sentence. • **also** (3) *after* / *before* a main verb ('cook', 'play', etc.) or (4) *after* / *before* 'be'.
Sequencing ideas	• **firstly**, **secondly**, or **finally** at the (5) *beginning* / *end* of a sentence.

b Which four linkers need a comma (,) afterwards?

__________ __________
__________ __________

3 Choose <u>one</u> of the charities below. Write an email asking for information about volunteering.

- Say why you're interested in volunteering. Give two or more reasons.
- Ask three questions.
- Use at least four different linkers.

WILD PARK ANIMAL CENTRE

OLYMPICS SPORT EVENT

HELP THE ELDERLY CHARITY

STRATEGY Use a variety of linkers to add or list ideas. This makes your writing more interesting and easier to read. Don't just use *and*!

PROGRESS TEST 2

GRAMMAR & VOCABULARY (25 points)

1 Choose the correct option to complete the conversation. *(4 points)*

A Hi, Jas. (0)... to the party later?

B Hmm. I'm not sure. I (1)... go, but I'm quite busy at the moment. I've got a Maths exam next week, so I'm revising. I hate Maths! It's my (2)... subject. I've already studied (3)... three hours this morning, and it's *still* impossible!

A Well, don't work all weekend. You (4)... take some breaks, too!

0	a Are you going	b Will you go	c You are going
1	a will	b might	c can
2	a worst	b worse	c bad
3	a for	b while	c since
4	a might	b have	c should

2 Complete the second sentence so that it has a similar meaning to the first. Use the word in **bold**. *(10 points)*

0 I don't know how to speak French.
I *have* *never* *studied* French. **STUDIED**

1 Smoking in this building is illegal.
You ________ ________ in here. **MUSTN'T**

2 Some people think Physics is more difficult than Biology or Chemistry.
Some people think Physics is ________ ________ ________ science subject. **THE**

3 Don't come to the barbecue if you don't want to.
You ________ ________ ________ come to the barbecue. **HAVE**

4 I am playing football later.
I am ________ ________ ________ football later. **GOING**

5 We moved here in 2005.
We ________ ________ here ________ 2005. **LIVED**

3 Write the words in the box in the correct column. *(6 points)*

bills course degree divorced gardening headache housework infection kindergarten married masters painkiller retire

Illness	Education	Life stages	Home life
			bills

4 Complete the sentences with the correct form of the words in brackets. *(5 points)*

0 Be *careful*! Look where you're going. *(care)*

1 Mrs Pantos is a middle-________ woman of around 50. *(age)*

2 This guidebook is really ________. It includes lots of information and maps. *(use)*

3 I don't like sad films. I always feel really ________ afterwards! *(depress)*

4 ________ people often live on the streets. *(home)*

5 Today's lesson was really ________. *(interest)*

READING (25 points)

1 Read the webpage and complete the summary about Leo Gatiss. *(3 points)*

Leo is a retired head (1)________ from (2)________ who now works in (3)________.

Volunteer story: **Leo Gatiss**

(0) *b*

I work with several primary schools in Ghana, helping teachers to plan courses and mark exams. I have to travel a lot, so I've bought a very old motorcycle. It's very noisy, and it isn't very fast, but it's reliable – and the children laugh when they see a middle-aged teacher from New Zealand arriving in a cloud of smoke!

(1) ____

I was the head teacher of a big primary school in New Zealand. I retired early, in my fifties, then I discovered that I was bored. I didn't want to do gardening, or join a golf club, like lots of my friends. I wanted a new challenge.

(2) ____

Easy in some ways, and difficult in others. Everyone has been very welcoming, and I've made wonderful friends. But many schools don't have computers, or even many books. Teachers have to be very creative.

(3) ____

I've been here for three years, ten months and nine days!

(4) ____

Working with the children, of course, and exploring the beautiful countryside, especially the coast. I'm not as keen on the forests. I always seem to get lost! I also volunteer at a local hospital. I'm not a doctor, but I help the nurses to give out painkillers, take X-rays, and so on. I like feeling useful.

(5) ____

That's a difficult question! I've fallen in love with Ghana, but I miss my family too. I want to stay here for at least two more years, if I can. But we'll see.

2 Match questions a–g to 0–5 in the webpage. There is one question that you don't need. *(10 points)*

a What are you going to do next?
b ~~What do you do now?~~
c What did you do before?
d What is your job like?
e How long have you been a volunteer?
f Why should people volunteer?
g What do you enjoy the most?

3 Are the sentences true (T) or false (F)? Correct the false sentences. *(12 points)*

0 Leo doesn't travel very quickly. (T) / F
______
1 Leo doesn't enjoy working in the garden as a hobby. T / F
______
2 Students study IT in most schools in Ghana. T / F
______
3 Leo has been in Ghana for nearly four years. T / F
______
4 Leo prefers the forests to the beaches. T / F
______
5 Leo has a degree in medicine. T / F
______
6 Leo's family don't live in Ghana. T / F
______

LISTENING *(25 points)*

1 T2 Listen to three conversations. Where does Zeinab work? *(1 point)*

a secondary school / a college / a university

2 Complete the questions with the missing words. Listen again and check. *(12 points)*

0 Which instruments *can* you play?
1 ______ time should I arrive?
2 How ______ does a course here cost?
3 ______ old are the students here?
4 ______ I have to have any qualifications?
5 ______ can I park?
6 ______ you been to the area before?

3 Listen again. Choose the correct replies to the questions in **2**. *(12 points)*

0 a piano and drums (b) guitar and drums c guitar and piano
1 a 6.15 b 6.30 c 7.30
2 a nothing b £40 c £75
3 a 16–96 b 14–70 c 15–68
4 a a school leaving certificate b none c a degree
5 a next to the supermarket b next to the petrol station c next to the park
6 a No, never. b Yes, regularly. c Yes, a few times.

WRITING *(25 points)*

1 Read the web post. Who is the person writing? *(2 points)*

> help! Ive just started a french course at university. Its very stressful. I work for long hours, and i feel tired and ill. What should I do.

2 Rewrite the web post in **1**. Correct five more punctuation mistakes. *(5 points)*

Help! ______
______
______
______

3 Choose the correct options to complete the reply. *(3 points)*

> (0) *(Firstly,) / What's more,* I think you should try to relax. It's only the start of the course, so you have a lot of time to study. When I started my degree, I (1) *also / as well* felt quite stressed, but after a while it got easier. It'll get better for you as well! (2) *Finally, / Secondly,* I think you're probably working too hard. You (3) *can't / shouldn't* work for long hours every day. It isn't healthy! Why (4) *don't / not* you phone some friends and plan some fun activities (5) *also / too?* (6) *End, / Finally,* I'm worried about your health. You should go to bed early, take regular exercise and eat well. If you still feel ill, you should see a doctor. You might need medical advice.
>
> I wish you lots of luck. I hope you feel better soon.

4 Read the web post below and write a reply. Include at least three pieces of advice. *(15 points)*

> Help! I'm 28, and I work in a supermarket. I don't have much money, so I still live with my parents. I'd like a new job, but I don't have any qualifications. What should I do? I'm really interested in computers.

1.1, *p. 3, Ex 7*

A **A:** I've got an email from Hernan. He isn't coming to the football game today.
B: What? But we always play football on Saturdays.
A: It's not his fault. His parents are having some old friends round. One of them is a journalist in Egypt. She's bilingual – she speaks English and Arabic. Hernan wants to talk to her about her job.
B: Does he want to be a journalist then?
A: Yeah! That's his dream job. He writes a blog for the university magazine already.

B **C:** Mum!
D: What is it, Jackie? I'm busy. I'm reading the newspaper.
C: I'm bored. I want to go roller-blading in the park, but it's raining.
D: Well, there are lots of things to do indoors.
C: Like what?
D: Well, your brother's surfing the Internet. Why don't you do that with him?
C: No, I don't want to. He's only sending emails. He isn't doing anything fun.
D: Well, what about listening to music?
C: No. I want to phone my friend Tina, but Dad's talking to someone on the phone.

1.2, *p. 6, Exs 2 & 3*

1 **I** = interviewer **S** = Sara
I: So, what languages do you speak, Sara?
S: Spanish – I'm from Vigo, in Spain. And, uh, English, of course! Um... that's all!
I: OK... So, what do you think about New York?
S: I love it! I go out all the time. There's very much... I mean, uh, there's loads to do! I really like going clubbing, and listening to music at concerts. Oh, and I love shopping. New York is great for shops. My favourite is the big... uh... what do you call a big shop that sells lots of different things?
I: Do you mean a department store?
S: That's it! I love Macy's department store. And I like...

2 **I** = interviewer **K** = Keito
I: Thank you for coming, Keito. Now, we have a lot of international visitors here. How many languages do you speak?
K: Well, I'm bilingual in English and Japanese, and I speak good French too.
I: Good. And what kind of person are you, Keito? What do you enjoy doing in your free time?
K: I like playing sport, especially in Central Park in summer. I also like shopping, and eating out at restaurants. I know lots of good restaurants in New York.
I: That could be very useful!

3 **I** = interviewer **R** = Roos
I: So, er, Roos, where are you from?
R: I'm from Holland, and I speak Dutch, English, German, French and Spanish.
I: Wow! That's a lot!
R: Oh, and uh, I speak some Italian, too.
I: Fantastic! What do you like doing, Roos?
R: I am a hard worker and...
I: No, I mean, what do you like doing in your free time?
R: Free time? Well, I like surfing the internet.
I: OK. And anything else?
R: Um... I like having friends round. I don't usually go out much.
I: I see, OK...

2.2, *p. 12, Exs 1 & 2*

Caye Caulker is a tiny island in the Caribbean, just 50 kilometres south of Mexico. And some people say it's the most relaxing place in the world. The official motto of the island is 'Go Slow', because nothing happens quickly there! I spent a week on the island with my family last August, and found it to be incredibly peaceful and easy-going. But at the same time, it was never boring.

It's impossible to feel stressed on Caye Caulker. The locals are very friendly and welcoming, and there's no traffic noise, because – amazingly – there aren't any cars. You don't even need to cook, because the food at the seafood restaurants is cheap as well as delicious. And the island is perfect for lazy Canadian tourists like me, because the main language on the island is English, although some locals speak Spanish, too.

The island is sunny and warm, but not hot. Thanks to the cooling winds from the east, it's possible to spend all day outdoors. And you won't want to stay in! The island is beautiful. We swam in the blue sea, and spent lots of time taking it easy on a white, sandy beach. We also enjoyed fishing, sailing, and simply exploring the beautiful island and watching the birds. The wildlife here is really colourful, and we took some wonderful photos.

Is Caye Caulker the most relaxing place in the world? We'd love to hear your views. Call us on...

3.1, *p. 14, Ex 4*

M = Masako **J** = Jim
1 **M:** So, Jim, let's start our tour of my city, Kyoto.
J: It's beautiful, Masako.
M: Many people think that Kyoto is the most beautiful city in Japan. It was the capital city in the past.
J: I didn't know that. So what is this building?
M: This is a tower. The Yasaka Pagoda.
J: Wait a moment. I'll take a photo.

2 **M:** Here is the Toji Temple. It's a very famous Buddhist temple.
J: How old is it, Masako?
M: It's about 1,300 years old. It's a very important religious monument in our country.

3 **J:** What an amazing place!
M: We're in the Imperial Park here. That building is Kyosho Gosho. It was a palace and it was built for the Emperor of Japan.
J: Can we visit it?
M: Yes, we can!

4 **M:** I often come here to relax. It's called the Philosopher's Walk. You can walk along the river and you can cross the bridge to see some interesting buildings on the other side.
J: The Philosopher's Walk?
M: It's named in memory of a professor at the university. He walked here every day when he was alive.

5 **J:** This is the town cemetery?
M: Yes, people come here to bury the dead. I brought you here to show you the statue of Buddha.
J: It's very impressive. You have a fabulous city, Masako.

3.4, *p. 18, Exs 1 & 2*

I = interviewer **M** = Maruschka
I: Hi! I'm talking to the well-known actress and writer, Maruschka Valentin, about her new book, 'The Fame Game.' Hello, Maruschka.
M: Hello.
I: I'd love to be famous! But I don't think I've got a good face for TV.
M: Really? I don't agree! Think of people like Al Pacino, Bill Gates or Barbara Streisand. They're famous because they're interesting and very talented. Not because they're beautiful supermodels!
I: That's true. But some of my friends think that looks are important.
M: Hmm... maybe you need some nicer friends! Don't worry about other people's opinions too much. Celebrities need to be very confident!
I: So, what can I do if I want to be famous?
M: First of all, decide what you want to be famous *for*. In my opinion, it's a mistake to go on reality TV shows. People who try to become a celebrity this way usually aren't famous for long! Get a celebrity boyfriend, girlfriend or even just a friend if you can – that does help! But best of all, try to be famous for being you. Do something you enjoy, and work hard. But don't work every day. I think it's important to have a life, too!

I: Interesting... And what's your top tip?
M: It's probably this: advertise yourself! Post online videos, have your own website, give interviews. Make sure people know your name. And keep watching or reading the news to find out what people are saying about you.
I: Thank you, Maruschka, that's fascinating. And I wish you lots of success with your book...

T1, *p. 21, Exs 1 & 2*

P = presenter **I** = interviewer
P: Today we ask: is London the most multilingual city in the world? Our research says that Londoners speak more than 350 languages! What's more, more than 1 million people in London don't speak English at home. That includes 41% of all school students. So what languages are we speaking? We went to find out.
I: Excuse me. Do you have a moment?
A: Sure.
I: Can you tell me, what languages do you speak?
A: Uh, well, I speak English when I'm here in London. But I'm from Morocco, so I also speak Arabic and... some French. Arabic is the only official language in Morocco but a lot of people there speak French.
I: I see. Did you know that French is the second biggest language in the UK, too? About 23% of British people know some French.
A: Really? No, I didn't know that...
B: When I'm at home with my family, I speak Hindi. But when I'm at university, or out with my friends, I always speak English.
I: Are there a lot of international students at your university?
B: Yes, definitely! I don't feel lonely. I think I read somewhere that there are over, uh, 87,000 international students at London universities, so I don't think...
C: Uh... I'm from China, so I speak Mandarin. My English is not very good because, err, I don't live in London. I'm a tourist!
I: Oh, OK. Do you like the city?
C: Yes, it's very nice.
P: Thanks, Tom. And as that last speaker reminds us, London is also a major tourist destination, with more than 13 million international visitors a year. So...

4.1, *p. 23, Ex 8*

1 **A:** Harry! Can you help me do the housework, please?
B: Sorry, Mum. I'm going out. I do karate on Saturday afternoons, remember?
A: Oh! So I have to do everything, do I?

2 **D:** Hello, Julia. How are you?
C: Everything's going well, thank you, Sue. My granddaughter got married at the weekend.
D: Did she? Who's the lucky man?

3 **F:** How was your weekend, Paul?
E: Good, thanks! I went fishing with my dad yesterday, and we caught an enormous fish. A salmon.
F: Wow! Really? Are you going to cook it?
E: No, we didn't kill it. We put it back in the river.

4 **G:** Is something wrong, Kim?
H: Yeah, my daughter left home at the weekend to go to university. I miss her already.
G: Oh, don't worry. She'll be back to visit soon!
H: Thanks, Alan. I'm sure you're right.

5 **I:** Are you enjoying the knitting class, Louise?
J: No! It's too difficult for me. I'm not very good at doing crafts. I've decided to stop the class.
I: Me too – I don't like it!

6 **K:** Otto! I've got some news! My sister is going to have a baby!
L: Great news! Congratulations, Bill. I didn't know they wanted to have children.
K: Yeah, they do. They love kids. It's so exciting.

4.2, *p. 26, Exs 1 & 2*

C = Chavez **K** = Karina
C: Welcome back, Karina! I've missed you.
K: Hi, Chavez! It's great to see you again! So tell me, how's it going?
C: Not bad, thanks! How are things with you?
K: Great, thanks! I've got lots to tell you. It's been a long time since we last met!
C: Let's go and have lunch. I want to hear everything!
The next train to arrive at Platform 2A will be the 11.45 service to Union Station, Los Angeles.

4.3, *p. 26, Exs 1–3*

1 **A:** Oh Gabe, I'm so proud. My son, the doctor!
B: Oh stop it Mom! I haven't even started the course yet.
A: I know, I know... Well, have a good journey. Call me when you get there.
B: Of course. But don't worry, I'll be fine!

2 **A:** Turn left here, Christa... Now go straight on, past the hospital... Slow down!
B: Sorry! Is this better?
A: Much better. Now, why don't you park just here, behind that red car.

3 **A:** And when you've finished in here, please start in the kitchen.
B: In there?
A: Right. Thanks, David. You're doing a great job. You're much faster than the last guy who worked here!

4 **A:** Please, take a card, Mrs Amusa. There are six names on the card, one for each candidate. Put a cross next to one name only.
B: Excuse me, what do I do when I've finished?
A: Put your card in this box, and go out through the door on the right.

5 **A:** Congratulations, Mara! So, did you get any good presents?
B: I got some amazing presents. Mum and Dad bought me a car! I've got lessons next week.
A: Wow! I guess you're all grown-up now then...
B: Yeah, thanks, cousin! You're only two years older than me, remember?!

5.1, *p. 28, Ex 4*

1 **A:** What did you do at school today, Katie?
B: We learnt about Aristotle and Plato. They had some amazing ideas, two and a half thousand years ago!
A: Yeah, that's right. I studied Plato on my degree course at university.

2 **A:** My daughter is learning French, now.
B: That's good, isn't it?
A: But she's only six years old! She's at primary school. I didn't study subjects like that at her age.
B: No, but it's a good idea. You learn more quickly when you're very young.

3 **A:** I just don't understand it. All this information about money and companies. Who's interested in that?
B: My brother. He's doing a masters in Economics. It's a one-year course. He loves it!
A: Well, I think it's boring! I don't think I'm going to get very good marks in this exam.

4 **A:** Hi Sandra, how are you feeling?
B: A lot better, thanks. I was really ill yesterday! Did I miss anything at college?
A: Um, we started learning *Romeo and Juliet*. You know, the Shakespeare play? We're going to do a performance at the high school!

5 **A:** Frida is brilliant with computers. She's the best programmer that I've ever taught.
B: Is she going to study programming at university when she leaves school?
A: Yeah, but I don't know what they're going to teach her. She's so good!

6 **A:** That's a good picture, Tom.
B: It's a map of India. We have to do it for our homework.
A: I see. You're learning some interesting things now you're at secondary school.

5.3, *p. 30, Ex 2*

You have five new messages. Message 1.

A: Oh, it's Anna here. I'm sorry but I can't come tonight. I'm meeting my kids after kindergarten, then it's dinner time, bath time. You know. Sorry, Alex.

Message 2.

B: Alex! It's me, Bob. Yeah, I'm free. I want to come out. Where are we going to meet? Call me any time. Bye.

Message 3.

C: Err... Hi, err... It's Danny. I don't know where I'm going to be this evening. I'll call or text you or something. Is that OK? Um... yeah. Bye.

Message 4.

D: Hi Alex, it's Carmen. I got your message. Well, Judy and I are doing our Art class tonight from six to eight. But we're free after that. Call me.

Message 5.

E: It's Laura. I'm studying in the library this evening, all evening, so I can't meet this time. Sorry, Alex. Bye for now.

End of messages.

5.4, *p. 32, Exs 1–3*

1 **A:** You've always been the clever one. Even when we were children, you always got the best marks.

B: That isn't true! We were just different. I was always much better at Languages and History than Maths – and you were the opposite. And I was never any good at sport. Dad was always really proud of your success, there.

A: You're right. Do you remember when I beat cousin Lola in that race? Dad couldn't stop smiling...

2 **A:** Well, to summarise... your speaking is excellent, but your writing needs more work. Your marks for listening aren't bad, and your reading is much better.

B: I've done more practice this month.

A: It shows!

B: But I want to get better before the exam. My manager says I have to pass! Could you give me some extra exercises to work on at home?

A: Of course! Come and see me after the next class.

3 **A:** Congratulations on winning the competition! So, tell us, what's the secret of your success?

B: You want my opinion? It isn't so much natural skill, or even confidence, although that's essential, too. It's mainly about how much work you do – oh, and a little bit of luck. To be the best, you need to train for five days a week. Less than that, and you can forget about winning races. More than that isn't healthy, and you'll end up going to see the doctor.

6.3, *p. 38, Exs 1–3*

T = Tiago **L** = Lorna

T: Hello?

L: Hi Tiago, it's Lorna. Good news!

T: What?

L: A journalist and a photographer are coming! The paper's going to publish an article about the party.

T: No way! Really?

L: It's true. And they're going to give a hundred dollars, too.

T: Wow. That's great news! Thanks Lorna, you're a star.

L: No problem. Listen, it's eleven now. I'll be at yours in about an hour?

T: Great – see you!

T = Tiago **M** = mother

T: Hello?

M: Tiago, it's your mother.

T: Oh, hi, Mum.

M: Now about tonight. What should I wear? I first thought my black dress, but your father said it was a bit serious.

T: Oh, err...

M: And then I thought, maybe jeans and a nice top? But is that too informal? Tiago?

T: Yes, uh, sorry Mum. You can wear any clothes you like. Remember that there's going to be a band, so wear something comfortable for dancing. Listen Mum, I'm quite busy at the moment, can I call you later?

M: Of course. Bye for now, then. Oh, wait – what time does it start?

T: 7.30. Bye, Mum!

T = Tiago **S** = Samir

T: Again? Hello?

S: Hi. It's Samir. Tiago, we've got a problem. Our car broke down.

T: Oh no! That's awful.

S: And we've got all the food and drinks for tonight in the back!

T: Where are you?

S: Opposite the stadium, on Green Road.

T: No problem – I'll pick you and the food up. Wait there!

T2, *p. 41, Exs 1–3*

1 **Z** = Zeinab **A** = customer 1

Z: Good morning, how can I help you?

A: I'd like to join a music class.

Z: Certainly. Which instruments can you play?

A: The guitar, and I'm not bad on the drums. But I'd like to learn the piano. I've never played it before.

Z: Then I recommend Susie Browne's Tuesday evening class. The piano is her speciality!

A: Oh, great! So, what time should I arrive?

Z: 6.30... no, sorry, I mean a quarter past six. Each class is two hours long, with a break at half past seven.

A: And how much does a course here cost?

Z: £40, or just £75 for two courses. And there's a free end-of-term concert trip, which...

2 **Z** = Zeinab **B** = customer 2

B: Hello. I'd like to join your IT beginners' class.

Z: Certainly.

B: I'm 68, and I never went to university. How old are the students here?

Z: Anywhere up to 96! Our youngest students are 16, but don't worry, I think there are 14 or 15 students here over 70, so you certainly won't be the oldest.

B: Oh good. And do I have to have any qualifications?

Z: You don't need to have a degree, or even a school leaving certificate. Although we can help you study for a variety of qualifications, if you wish...

3 **Z** = Zeinab **C** = customer 3

Z: Hello, Zeinab speaking.

C: Good afternoon. I'm starting a sculpture course here next week, and I'm travelling by car. Where can I park?

Z: We don't have a car park here, unfortunately, but there's one nearby, opposite the park, on the left of the supermarket. There's a petrol station five minutes away. Have you been to the area before?

C: Once or twice, but I've forgotten it. I've never been very good at Geography!

Until last year, I hated computer games. I didn't know much about them, and what I saw, I didn't like. When Oli was late for dinner, or got bad marks for homework, I blamed his love of computer games. To me, computers were bad. After a day at work sending emails and surfing the internet, the last thing I wanted to do is come home and switch on again for fun.

That is, not until a friend introduced me to *Spore*. I started playing as a joke, but soon I found I was logging in regularly. What I liked about *Spore* is that it wasn't about killing or hurting people. In *Spore*, you create new animals, and then you help them to grow, evolve, and eventually build their own homes and cities. It's fascinating. I've always loved Biology, but this game made me think about History and Politics too. It was lots of fun. I loved inventing my own animals. My favourite was pink and purple, and had 42 eyes! After a while, I forgot I was sitting at a computer. One day I was even late for dinner. Oli thought that was very funny!

TRANSCRIPT	CONTENT	TRACK
1.1	Page 3, Exercise 7	1
1.2	Page 6, Listening, Exercises 2 & 3	2
2.1	Page 9, Exercise 5	3
2.2	Page 12, Listening, Exercises 1 & 2	4
3.1	Page 14, Exercise 4	5
3.2	Page 15, Exercise 7	6
3.3	Page 18, Functional language, Exercises 1 & 2	7
3.4	Page 18, Listening, Exercises 1 & 2	8
T1	Page 21, Progress test 1, Listening	9
4.1	Page 23, Exercise 8	10
4.2	Page 26, Functional language, Exercises 1 & 2	11
4.3	Page 26, Listening, Exercises 1–3	12
5.1	Page 28, Exercise 4	13
5.2	Page 29, Exercise 8	14
5.3	Page 30, Exercise 2	15
5.4	Page 32, Listening, Exercises 1–3	16
6.1	Page 34, Exercise 4	17
6.2	Page 38, Functional language, Exercise 2	18
6.3	Page 38, Listening, Exercises 1–3	19
T2	Page 41, Progress test 2, Listening	20

Notes